The Burden of Excellence

The Burden of Excellence

The struggle to establish the Preuss School UCSD and a call for urban Educational Field Stations

by
Cecil Lytle

Plowshare Media

LA JOLLA, CALIFORNIA

Copyright © 2008 by Cecil Lytle
All rights reserved
Printed in the United States of America

Library of Congress Control Number: 2010924042
Lytle, Cecil
The Burden of Excellence

ISBN: 978-0-615-20746-9

First Printing May 2008
Second Printing September 2010

Published by RELS Press, a non-profit imprint of:
Plowshare Media
P.O. Box 278
La Jolla, CA 92038
RELS.UCSD.EDU

PUBLISHER'S NOTE

Without limiting the rights under copyright reserved above,
no part of this publication may be reproduced, stored in or introduced
into a retrieval system, or transmitted, in any form, or by any means
(electronic, mechanical, photocopying, recording or otherwise),
without the prior written permission of the author.
For information about permission to
reproduce selections of this book, contact:

Permissions, Plowshare Media, P.O. Box 278, La Jolla, CA 92038
or visit PLOWSHAREMEDIA.COM

*To all of the women, men, and children
who believe that making change for the better
is the reason we were put here on earth.*

Contents

Preface......*ix*

I. Campus and Conscience......1

II. Anatomy of an Argument......13

III. Death by a Thousand Committees......37

IV. Enter the White House......63

V. Ashes, Ashes......83

VI. Preuss School UCSD......101

Acknowledgements......137

Preface

Like most trends, the national clash over affirmative action began in California. The epicenter was the race and gender consciousness in the admissions policy of the University of California (UC). The 1978 *Regents of the University of California v. Bakke* United States Supreme Court decision allowed the university to continue preferential admissions policies for African Americans and Latinos, but without quotas. It was a decision without a conclusion, a legal and semantic conundrum. Opposition to affirmative action in UC admissions continued to mount in direct proportion to the competition for seats in the freshman class at the most selective UC campuses. A generation later in 2005, the clash came to pit two seemingly virtuous principles against one another: the liberal instincts of the faculty and administration for a well-educated, diverse populace and the conservative kidnapping of the jargon of fairness on behalf of beleaguered, affluent whites and Asians, sensing slippage in their paths to opportunity in a state once thought to be forever golden. An uneasy truce settled over the state as standardized test scores and high school grade point averages inexorably became the overarching criteria determining merit and admission to the University of California.

The anti-affirmative action movement in California was led by African American businessman Ward Connerly, a UC regent appointed by Republican Governor Pete Wilson. Theirs was a two-step process: first in 1995, Wilson and Connerly led the University of California regents to narrowly pass a resolution, Special Provision 1 (SP-1), that forbade the use of race or gender in the university's admissions process. SP-1 was carefully crafted and aimed to unabashedly cut off any liberal-leaning contrivances that might include considerations of race or gender in the UC admissions process. Each word, line, paragraph, and section anticipated and choked off the future creation of any possible loopholes around the regulation. It passed by a relatively narrow 14-10 vote, with 1 abstention. This new university provision was coupled with Executive Order W-124-95, signed by Governor Pete Wilson to, "End preferential treatment and to promote individual opportunity based on merit." Here, for the first time, was clear evidence that the opponents of affirmative action were beginning to put in place contravening regulatory structures that would systematically do what the *Bakke* decision had failed to do, namely, eliminate affirmative action from the UC admissions process.

The following year, during the national election that saw California turn to Bill Clinton by a 2-to-1 margin, Wilson and Connerly engineered the passage of statewide Proposition 209 which disallowed any consideration of race or gender in governmental matters. Their campaign aimed to vouchsafe opportunity and advancement for citizens immediately positioned to exploit them. It did not, however, address how a sympathetic government or its universities might help equalize the doorways and playing fields available to youngsters not given a head start by their parents, schools, and race.

As the University of California faced the twenty-first century, the institution stood mute regarding its capability and responsibility to help the multitude of young people whose families could not overcome the historical disadvantages of their compromised socio-economic circumstances and race.

Several of the campuses sought different methods to enroll students from groups that were historically underrepresented in the freshman class. Richard Atkinson, newly elected president of the University of California after the passage of SP-1, in 1995, suffered a very public spanking from Governor Wilson after mentioning that he thought that the anti-affirmative action provision was only advisory. Most initial attempts by the campuses sought to circumvent the new exclusionary policy by asserting a "comprehensive review" of UC applications in the hope of adding extra admission points for personal attributes characterizing disadvantage in order to help tilt the admissions game enough to make more disadvantaged youngsters eligible for admission.

Despite this "thumb on the scale" approach, the effort failed to enroll a significant number of high school graduates from disadvantaged backgrounds. UC campuses with less rigorous academic requirements and reputations took in most of the few African American and Latino students admitted under the "comprehensive review" scheme. It remained the case, however, that the more rigorous academic admissions requirements for Berkeley, UCLA, and UC San Diego prohibited enrollment of sizeable numbers of students of color deemed eligible even after "comprehensive review."

During the years immediately following SP-1, enrollment of Latino and African American students dropped by one-third to one-half, depending on the campus. Reasons for the decline centered on three theories. First, many felt that minority students were put off by the affirmative action debate and simply chose not to apply. A second notion claimed that even after minority students were accepted, the actual yield rate among these students fell away due to attractive admit offers from selective private universities. Yet others believed that the elimination of affirmative action simply made fewer low-income minority students eligible. There is some truth in each of these explanations for the decline in minority enrollments.

UC San Diego was in the most precarious position of all the ten general campuses regarding diversity. The absence of big-time football and basketball, as well as the urban attractions of the Bay Area and Los Angeles, made the scenic La Jolla campus less attractive and less relevant to low-income urban high school graduates.

Those precious few competitively eligible minority students from the inner city were heavily recruited by the elite private universities. If these students preferred one of the highly selective state universities, they would most often choose the urban settings of UCLA or Berkeley over San Diego.

The establishment of the Preuss School UCSD, a college preparatory charter school on the UCSD campus, was the beginning of the fulfillment of a commitment to the preservation of the twin virtues of academic excellence and social responsibility. The model school we wished to build would serve as an example of what the future of urban education could be. This initiative aimed to properly identify and attack the root causes of disparity in educational outcomes.

Despite enthusiastic support from the targeted communities, the effort met with surprisingly stiff opposition from the UCSD faculty. That opposition centered on three concerns: Was the running of such an on-campus charter school within the mission of the university? Were children from poor disadvantaged backgrounds capable of overcoming educational deficits to achieve academic excellence? And, were the costs too high?

The very public argument over eliminating affirmative action in California was an ugly debate that pitted one race against another. Despite the high-minded rhetoric about racial neutrality, whites and Asians felt, with good reason, that the admission of underqualified blacks and Latinos would occur at the expense of their group's opportunities. The effort to establish an on-campus secondary charter school dedicated to preparing low-income students of color for college took place amid the idyllic and polysyllabic polite parlance of a public research university. This local debate is an aspect of the broader national debate over race, class, and privilege.

Underneath the superb speeches and numerous faculty votes, however, raged the ancient struggle between the "haves" and "have nots."

This is the story of that struggle.

Chapter One

Campus and Conscience

The Land-Grant Gift

From their start in the early 1960s, the undergraduate colleges at the University of California, San Diego (UCSD) grew along the path of Gilman Drive, a serpentine tree-lined road hugging the cliffs of La Jolla with stunning Pacific overlooks. As the campus developed over the next four decades, Gilman came to divide the gray stone monolithic buildings of the School of Medicine from the remnant Quonset huts and barracks of Camp Matthews, an old military base hastily erected by the United States Marines right after the attack on Pearl Harbor.

The early campus was dotted with abandoned guard posts and concrete-reinforced machine gun bunkers from a time when it was feared that an enemy might climb the La Jolla bluffs to invade America. These unused relics of war stood in stark relief against the modern campus that was emerging from a twentieth century vision of progress and enlightenment.

Few are aware that it was the street's namesake, Daniel Coit Gilman, who fathered the concept of the public land-grant university in the nineteenth century. His was an energetic vision of America that endured across a civil war, two world wars, and several cold war skirmishes. It was a vision of how America could best use its natural and human resources in the interest of the nation's burgeoning economic development.

The land-grant movement, begun with passage of the Morrill

Act in 1862, invested in over one hundred institutions of higher learning in order to propel the intellectual and economic development of a young America, still in the throes of manifest destiny. Those nascent egalitarian impulses led to the founding of the National Schools of Science and dozens of agriculture and mining schools, as well as teachers' and women's colleges in nineteen states.

It took a second iteration of the Morrill Act in 1890 to extend this government-sponsored educational franchise to the untapped potential of the newly freed African American population, with the founding of such institutions as Tuskegee University, Alabama A&M, North Carolina A&T, and many others. This second group of land-grant colleges and universities, like the burgeoning women's colleges, was essentially an East Coast and southern phenomenon, separate and useful.

By the end of the Civil War, California was one of the newest states in the Union, free of slavery and absent any institutions of higher education targeting ethnic minority groups. The same case remains today. The University of California, therefore, became the singular hope for any excluded person wishing to emerge into the mainstream and the professions.

The University of California entered the period following World War II staking much of its reputation and future on the celebrity of the campus near Oakland, California. Taking its 1866 charter to heart, the faculty of the Berkeley campus mounted and sustained major research, as well as programs of instruction that conveyed direct and immediate benefit to the State of California and its citizens.

Most notably, the UC Agricultural Field Stations, dotted around the state, delivered on the faith and resources put into the state's public university system by developing and disseminating the research that has made agriculture one of the chief industries in California. The Agricultural Field Station is emblematic of the university's commitment to research, teaching, and service programs that directly aid the economic development and social tranquility of the state.

Scientific research in the emerging fields of plant technologies, animal husbandry, genetic engineering, and the macro-economics of agriculture has helped to make the California economy the seventh-largest in the world, and to transform the arid Central Valley from a desert into productive farmland. A hand-in-hand collaboration between statewide and federal governmental agricultural agencies became the benchmark for all future teaching and research programs at the University of California.

Based on the success of the UC Agricultural Field Station model, other UC/governmental collaborations have been nurtured under the aegis of the university's broader public mission. For example, faculty and researchers at the California Space Grant Consortium (Cal-Space) have aided the various missions of NASA. UC material science and structural engineering groups developed the solutions for the California Department of Transportation (Cal-Trans) that have gone into retrofitting California's freeways since the 1993 Northridge earthquake. The Lawrence Livermore National Laboratory grew out of the older UC Berkeley Radiation Lab and has served the U.S. Department of Energy's research and national security mission for more than 58 years. Clinical research at the five UC teaching hospitals has led to improvements in health care methodologies that can not be overstated on a world scale.

The Multiversity

UC Berkeley stood alone at the top of the state's educational food chain because, for the first half of the twentieth century, the Berkeley campus was the only four-year state sponsored university that granted doctoral degrees. Even UCLA struggled for years to throw off its diminutive moniker, "the Southern Branch," bestowed by administrators and colleagues who saw all UC expansion in terms of a pejorative relationship to the main campus by the bay. Aided by alumni and the media, the Berkeley campus of the University of California system still prefers to be known by its pop culture sobriquet, "Cal."

While several new UC campuses would be founded during the 1960s, UC Berkeley developed into a premier public research institution rivaling Harvard and Princeton under the leadership of Clark Kerr. A Stanford and Berkeley-trained labor economist, Kerr, after serving as chancellor of the Berkeley campus from 1952–58, was appointed president of the entire UC system.

Kerr's 1960 Master Plan for Higher Education laid out a three-tiered scheme for California's universities and colleges. The local community colleges were to have an open enrollment admissions policy serving the vocational and intellectual needs of students not readily admissible to the state's four-year institutions. Next, the California State University system would admit the top third of California's high school graduates and offer baccalaureate and some Master's level degrees. And finally, the institutions of the University of California would admit only the top 12.5% of each year's high school graduates and offer all levels of instruction, including doctoral and professional degrees.

The master plan delineated educational paths according to a student's demonstrated ability to learn and ability to pay. The focus was on the individual: Within the California university system, there would be an institution that met every student's abilities. The master plan was also a device to preserve special funding for the UC system at the expense of the other public systems for higher education in California.

The 1960 master plan set in motion a race for the top in which California families measured the potential of their children's future success by the attainment of a UC degree. Just one year after the master plan was unveiled, President Kennedy's Executive Order #10925 established the principle that encouraged preferential treatment for African American and other racial minorities. Even with the opening of three new campuses during the sixties, the first wave of baby boomers and newly enfranchised African Americans began to crowd the UC application process. These events inspired a series of outreach activities in higher education designed to recruit ethnic and racial minorities to the freshman class. For the next thirty years, social justice in the United States became inextricably linked to a seat in the most prestigious public universities and colleges.

While expanding the research power of the older UC campuses to rival European and East Coast models, Kerr took the plea of the university charter to heart. He understood, perhaps better than any university leader at the time, that both the prosperity and the tranquility of the state were largely dependent upon the presence of a well-educated populace. This meant that each campus would serve the state best by concentrating its resources and attention on meaningful undergraduate education, despite the portentous bulge of baby boomers making their way through California's secondary schools. (Interestingly, the UC campuses that Kerr had a direct hand in creating—San Diego, Irvine, and Santa Cruz—remain today the most heavily focused on the academic and social development of undergraduates.)

Although an academic, Kerr maintained a healthy distrust of the nexus of elitism and hubris in the public academy. Kerr felt in later years that the notoriety of the Berkeley campus led to a fundamental rupture in the social contract between the California public and its premier state university. Going into the 1960s, Berkeley's reputation with the common citizenry and the legislature it elected was as a bastion of theoretic extremity, elitism, aloofness, and acute insensitivity to the concerns of the common world outside Sather Gate.

For Kerr, the meteoric rise of the San Diego campus, too, came at a price. His memoirs reveal that he believed only the Santa Cruz campus remained faithful to his concept of the "Multiversity," devoted to nurturing young minds. Both the San Diego and Santa Cruz campuses were designed with undergraduates as the center of attention. Kerr developed each campus in the model of the premier English institutions (University of London, Cambridge, and Oxford) with small liberal arts colleges embedded in the larger campus.

Except for the establishment of Third College at UCSD in 1970, San Diego's faculty senate all but abandoned Kerr's notion of the campus' undergraduate colleges serving as the intellectual and resource engines driving the creation of the academic departments. In the desperate lurch to overtake UC Berkeley in prestige,

UCSD faculty interests quickly took precedence over the more student-based academic principles of the undergraduate colleges. A drive for excellence in research on the part of the faculty too often replaced concern for the achievement of UC's youngest students. By the 1980s, the success of Kerr's three experimental UC campuses was dependent on the understanding and goodwill of the University of California's tenured faculty.

The San Diego campus, in particular, was like a young gunfighter—lean and on the hunt for an earned reputation. Consequently, faculty self-interest gradually led UCSD to divert resources and attention from its undergraduate colleges to the academic departments. The success of the academic departments, in turn, rested heavily on the welfare of the faculty: their research, professional security (tenure), financial prosperity, and individual acclaim. Contrary to Kerr's vision, the educational philosophy of the San Diego campus assumed that a good undergraduate education was an automatic byproduct of an outstanding and well-funded faculty.

Meanwhile, upheavals on the Berkeley campus in the 1960s and 1970s were mirrored at other UC campuses: none were more notorious than the events taking place on the San Diego campus in idyllic La Jolla. The first real uproar at San Diego centered on the reappointment of Herbert Marcuse in the philosophy department at UCSD.

Problems in Paradise

Marcuse's curious background made him an unlikely hero for the New Left in the United States. Born a Jew in Germany, he fled his post at the Frankfort Institute for Social Research in 1934 to conduct research at Columbia University in New York. Perhaps because of his unorthodox blend of Freudian Marxism, he was never able to secure a permanent appointment at Columbia. With America's entry into World War II, he moved to Washington to work in various intelligence units, ultimately leading to his appointment as head of the Eastern European Section in the State Department where he stayed until 1950.

He was then appointed fulltime at Brandeis University. Upon his retirement at age 67 in 1965, the San Diego campus approached him for an adjunct appointment in its new and inchoate Department of Philosophy. The interested faculty felt that making such a senior and distinguished appointment in the humanities would help jumpstart the effort to balance UCSD's intellectual tilt toward the sciences. With him came his brilliant graduate student, Angela Davis.

His first books in English, *Reason and Revolution* and *Eros and Civilization* are barely penetrable tracts about an alternative organization of society that champions prosperity for the weak. Critics thumped his brand of social theory as rampant idealism at best, and nihilism at worst. His call for a new utopia made him a darling of America's New Left.

Angela Davis was his devoted and extremely articulate doctoral candidate and apprentice. Their burgeoning notoriety with the agitating elements of the New Left made them the nemeses of Governor Ronald Reagan. Marcuse was a social theorist with a particularly mischievous personal streak that electrified students. Although he seemed startled at first by his celebrity among young activist intellectuals, Marcuse became the figure that galvanized student protest on the San Diego campus.

Angela Davis figured prominently when the few African American and Latino students at UCSD put forth demands for a Marxist-inspired future college that would revolutionize all aspects of undergraduate education. In March of 1969, Davis gave a speech in which she recited what came to be known as the Lumumba-Zapata Demands. "Mexican Americans in the Southwest and black people in the industrial cities and the agrarian South continue to perform the dirty but necessary tasks of building a society of abundance, while systematically being denied the benefits of that society," she said. "Therefore," she continued, "we must reject the entire oppressive structure of America. Racism runs rampant in the educational system while America, in a pseudo-humanitarian stance, proudly proclaims that it is the key to equal opportunity for all. This is the hypocrisy our generation must now destroy."

She went on to read before more than seventy faculty, administrators, and black and brown student members of the Lumumba-Zapata Coalition specific demands for UCSD's proposed third undergraduate college. She outlined a plan for the new institution drawn by the students and their leftist faculty mentors, a plan including, among other things: 1) special admissions procedures to guarantee the enrollment of no less than 35% African American students, 35% Mexican American students, and other admissions controlled by a student committee; 2) a student controlled board of directors that had the power to hire and fire faculty; 3) Mexican and African influenced architecture for the new buildings that were to be built for the third UCSD undergraduate college; and, 4) the teaching of doctrinaire Marxist-Leninist theory and socialist revolutionary principles. Among the least negotiable of the demands was that the third UCSD college must be named Lumumba-Zapata College, jointly honoring the early twentieth century Mexican revolutionary, Emilio Zapata, and the assassinated Congolese African nationalist, Patrice Lumumba.

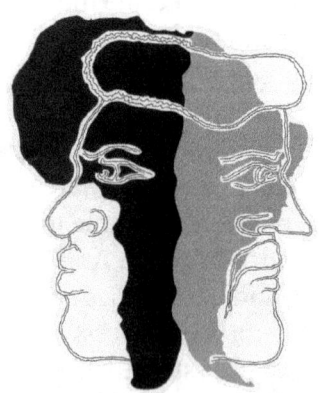

The drawing of Patrice Lumumba and Emilio Zapata that accompanied the front page article, "Third College–The Quiet Revolution" in the November 25, 1969 edition of the *UCSD Triton Times*.

Davis' vision of a new utopian campus in San Diego ushered in a collision between an institutional numbers-based meritocracy and the New Left populism now seeking a voice on the young campus.

Third College

The first two colleges had already successfully recruited freshmen classes drawn from the elite top 4% of California's high schools, not the full 12% as stipulated in the 1960 master plan devised by Clark Kerr. The most troubling demand for the university's legislative body of faculty and administrators, therefore, was that the next college would implement a separate admissions scheme that favored African American and Latino students. After some contention, an admissions policy for the proposed College III was finally agreed upon. Called the Background, Motivation, and Persistence Average, or BMPA, the plan was to create a subjective category that would measure and assign a numerical value to recognize and measure a student's motivation. Although an experiment, the BMPA lasted more than a decade, but it never spelled out the specific evidence of motivation or persistence. Students and then professional staff accepted the principle, but each recruiter and admissions officer was free to interpret what constituted motivation and persistence in high school.

On January 6, 1970, the UCSD Academic Senate met and quietly approved the BMPA without much discussion. However, in February, UCSD Chancellor William "Bill" McGill, withdrew any mention of the academic senate's approval of the BMPA when he sent the proposal to establish the third of UCSD's colleges to the UC regents for approval. Consequently, the newest college on the UCSD campus soon opened with an informal and separate admissions policy that was never approved by the UC regents, nor by Governor Ronald Reagan. Although UCSD's academic senate never explicitly accepted the special admissions program, Third College did succeed in opening in 1970 with approximately 70% of its students coming from the ranks of minority groups.

The liberal-leaning faculty essentially humored the students until they either graduated or flunked out. Gradually, over the duration of the presidencies of Jimmy Carter, Ronald Reagan, and George H.W. Bush, Third College slowly lost its initial utopian stridency to become more like any other U.S. college navigating the social complexities of the 1980s. Minority enrollments dropped as strictly academic admission standards rose.

In Search of Remedy and Reform

Throughout 1995 and 1996, University of California President Dick Atkinson grappled with both the short- and long-term fallout from SP-1. UC outreach efforts had been a dismal failure during the tenure of affirmative action in UC admissions policy. It was clear that without reform, employing the same efforts in isolation would still fail to recruit and graduate substantial numbers of underrepresented students. True educational reform had to be rooted in new initiatives aimed at overcoming the debilitating effects of subpar schooling in order to create a critical mass of competitively eligible young people in the inner-city core.

UC admission and graduation rates of ethnic minority students were never successful. At UCSD, for instance, the African American student population was never higher than four percent. Following the well-publicized elimination of affirmative action with SP-1, that number shrank by nearly half. UC efforts to retain a healthy population of underrepresented students were feeble and seemed designed more for favorable press releases than for genuine educational reform or true civic engagement.

The caustic debates taking place on the Berkeley campus during the 1960s revolved around the concerns of an awakened white middle class. Clashes over free speech, Vietnam, and People's Park spoke to the civil liberties of Berkeley students and sympathetic onlookers seeking further enfranchisement. The conflagration on the San Diego campus during the same period, however, was provoked by a blind institutional pursuit of elitism and the ensuing collision with the aspirations of African Americans and Latinos represented at Third College.

Is social responsibility the enemy of academic excellence? Are they competing virtues? Should the pursuit of academic superiority on the one hand convey a greater imperative on the other? Is there such a thing as a burden of excellence? The answers to these questions are deeply rooted in definitions of land-grant responsibility.

Academic Democracy

Unlike any other institution in modern western culture, the public university is a self-contained and ultimate democracy with its own rules of engagement and resolution. In no other civic forum are arguments formed with such precision and intensity, and in no other forum is each point of view, however strange, so well-protected from persecution. The public university, however, may also foster an abusive democracy where committees strangle initiatives with convoluted arguments and deliberations, where even the least perceptive faculty member in the room holds a veto. Campus debate usually pits the administration against the faculty and tends to strive for temporary consensus over terminal conclusion. It most often works because the participants choose between a series of alternatives that, over time, will speak to and satisfy their collective self-interests.

The public confers privileges upon the university and generally recognizes that the intellectual community provides services and solutions to large-scale societal problems over time. There are few regulations imposed on higher education by society. The university is left alone, for the most part, to devise and execute its own intimate procedures and is protected by the sanctity of academic freedom and tenure. These organizational privileges are not conferred upon any other social institution in western society.

A public research university, therefore, has the obligation to strengthen its academic program to serve the highest standards of achievement. To those within reach of a UC education, the institution conveys the promise of reward and opportunities for the future. For others, this promise remains unfulfilled.

Here was the paradox. Without major revision, the pursuit of institutional excellence would continue to take place at the expense of an equally important social responsibility. To meet these two seemingly incompatible goals, it would be necessary for the University of California to assume fully the burden of its excellence. A small group at UCSD's Third College—legatees of Marcuse and Davis—would call on the campus to lift that burden by remaining true to the ideals of Gilman and Kerr. This group would build an urban Educational Field Station.

No one could have known how painful it would be.

Chapter Two

Anatomy of an Argument

The founding of Third College and the implementation of the Background, Motivation, and Persistence Average (BMPA) brought a new institutional commitment to addressing the inequities inherent in public education. Third College proposed to level the playing field for highly motivated though otherwise disadvantaged students eager to enter the mainstream and compete. Although the BMPA was not sustainable, it demonstrated UCSD's willingness to be an agent of change. The task for Third College was to retain its social justice impetus in an environment that was increasingly becoming a competitive meritocracy based on superior test scores.

By 1988, Third College had all the earmarks of an institution still seeking a mature self-definition, following its painful birth pangs two decades earlier and successive years of adolescent drift. Members of the founding faculty were still around. Half complained that the other half had grown old, tired, or both, and had lost the radical vision of the early years. The progressives had clearly failed in their quest for a radical college. By the end of the eighties, the preferential admissions program for black, brown, and poor students had been abandoned and Third College's admission profile was exactly the same as that of the other UCSD colleges. The racial and socio-economic makeup of the student body had become whiter and richer. The core curriculum, once devoted to the study of the interior and exterior Third World, had now devolved into an odd mixture of discrete and unrelated courses in the sciences, mathematics, social sciences, humanities, and the arts.

The college's core course was called Societal Analysis. The faculty was led to adopt the course's title in dim homage to a revolutionary course called Social Analysis 139X, which Eldridge Cleaver was slated to teach at UCSD in 1968. As the campus continued to grow, various faculty, friendly and not-so-friendly, exploited a weakened college administration to demand that their pet courses be placed in the required line-up to bloat enrollments and help those faculty appear more necessary so they could secure tenure in their home departments.

The closing years of the eighties saw such petty collegiate dramas played out weekly in a social theater where conservative and progressive players glared at each other across the fault lines of ethnicity, spitting invectives in terms of "race," "preference," and "quotas." The number of African American and Latino students admitted by way of special consideration was dwindling, and those entering UCSD did not perform well or graduate in significant numbers. It was clear that the University of California was a flashpoint in the national affirmative action debate and that a new approach had to be found that would capture the altruistic aspirations of the civil rights movement and meet the mounting regressive impulses toward a strict numbers-based meritocracy that increasingly made a UC degree the sole property of the privileged.

That new approach came to be centered on the interventionist self-help advocacy of a UC-sponsored charter school that would prepare poor children for competitive college admission.

The effort to open such an on-campus charter school began in earnest with the passage of the 1992 California Charter School Act sponsored by Democratic State Senator Gary Hart from Santa Barbara. The provision followed similar legislation sprouting up in Michigan and 27 other states, and allowed the drafting of proposals for sponsorship of a charter school. Indeed, the measure encouraged an entity (parents, teachers, community organizations and others) to essentially subcontract with their local school district for the running of a particular school that would "break the mold" and provide a unique educational setting for those identified as "disadvantaged" students.

Unusual Suspects

Immediately, Third College hosted community forums disseminating the provisions of the Charter School Act. Senator Hart was invited by Third College to speak on campus to a broad San Diego audience. Hundreds of teachers, parents, and community activists crowded the forums to learn how they, too, might take advantage of this opportunity to improve the education of African American and Latino students. Within months, there appeared before the San Diego Unified School District several proposals to establish local charter schools.

Third College held numerous faculty meetings at which the notion of UCSD establishing a charter school for disadvantaged students was discussed. Except for a few incorrigible refugees from the 1960s, the faculty essentially ignored the idea. I mistakenly took their tepid response as a tacit endorsement of the project. This proved to be an error of judgment that would lead to all-out confrontation in the coming years.

Our effort became entangled in the raging California debate over affirmative action. Where Gilman might have stood on this issue one hundred years after championing the Land-Grant Movement is an interesting question. For five years, more than 2,300 pages of memos and reports were generated, hundreds of hours of meetings were logged, and countless e-mail messages flew across the campus, state, and nation. Very little other business got done while the University of California, San Diego sorted through its mail and its convictions.

After serving as the chair of UCSD's Department of Music, I was appointed provost of Third College in 1988. Given its history, no one would be surprised if I, as the chief academic officer of the college, continued pushing progressive issues. The campus had come to expect such behavior, and I certainly did not want to disappoint. I began to recruit members for a new UCSD Charter School Steering Committee.

My principal ally was sociology professor Hugh Mehan. Bud, as he preferred to be called, was the first faculty member hired by Third College in 1972 and his chief task was to establish and direct the UCSD Teacher Education Program. He joined me to help set up a steering committee to pull together research on the best practices in public education. We knew that the group had to be small and handpicked for their particular intellectual attributes and political acumen. Together, we would lead faculty and students in successfully pushing this effort through a phalanx of academic senate committees, campus administrators, community meetings, and, ultimately, the same University of California regents who had earlier turned their backs on minority students. His expertise and credentials as our card-carrying education expert were vital. He had written widely on what he termed the "hidden curriculum" in schools and how schools are designed to encourage the failure of African American and Latino students. He was not an instinctive fighter at first, but the hypocrisy and unrelenting attacks on his research made him a formidable champion of what seemed to be our lost cause.

Rafael Hernandez was essential. He instinctively understood poverty as a personal crucible and became a close confidant in the initiative. He had also felt the scourge of social disenfranchisement and decided that his professional life would be dedicated to empowering the powerless. As Third College's brilliant dean of students, Rafael had demonstrated his ability to work intelligently with upper middle-class kids from the suburbs while helping to lift the debilitating burden of discrimination from the shoulders of poor, Mexican American students who, against all odds, found themselves sitting in his office as UCSD students. He carried himself as a consummate gentleman whose charming ways masked a durable and enviable toughness. His skills were key to organizing UCSD students to serve as tutors, a critical element of our plan.

Patrick Ledden, a mathematician and provost of Muir College, was another obvious choice for the UCSD Charter School

Steering Committee. He was a long-time member of the faculty and was held in the highest esteem across the campus. A supremely elegant and ethical man, Pat had a fertile mind and gregarious temperament. When not teaching the poetry of calculus to daunted freshmen, he regularly taught an honors course on James Joyce's *Ulysses* for the literature department. Pat brought to the initiative his prodigious wisdom, political savvy, and an enormous amount of goodwill and trust. With Pat lending his calm demeanor to the committee, others could adopt more maverick ways to openly confront more obstreperous colleagues at meetings. For the most part, the strategy worked to perfection.

Joe Watson was a chemist who became the first provost of the fledgling Third College in 1968. Although he grew up just around the corner from me on Sugar Hill in New York City, we first met in La Jolla when I was appointed assistant professor in 1974. By the time the first proposal to establish the UCSD Charter High School had appeared for review, Joe was vice chancellor for student affairs and a wise, albeit cautious, counsel to the effort. Faustina Solis, Third College provost emeritus, also brought her powerful presence to the earliest sessions of our group.

The greatest asset of the UCSD Charter High School effort, however, was Bill McGill, a former UCSD chancellor. He had returned to the campus in the late 1980s to settle back in La Jolla following a harrowing tenure as president of Columbia University during a frightening and lethal ten-year period of political unrest. He had been the chancellor of UCSD in 1969 and on the receiving end of the Lumumba-Zapata Demands. During the early 1980s, he was UCSD Chancellor Richard Atkinson's confidant and mentor. During the 1990s, he became mine. Bill attended our monthly meetings faithfully. He chose to listen approvingly, but without much comment. Between meetings, I would drop in to his office for a chat. It was there that he guided me and shaped my thoughts about the prospects for a charter school and life. He became my coach. He did not pull punches. He scolded me if he thought I was too blunt in response to dissonance or too lenient with more agreeable allies. I looked forward to calling on him and was honored that he frequently walked over to my office to give his valued advice.

McGill was seduced by the UCSD Charter High School initiative as perhaps the last chance for him to get right a progressive agenda for higher education. He began to purge his demons through the writing of *Year of the Monkey*, a chronicle of his experiences as UCSD chancellor from 1968-70. Intuitively, Bill felt that the charter school effort might be his final opportunity to revisit the innocent ideals behind the founding of Third College and the Lumumba-Zapata Demands of 1969. I believe he felt he had a better instrument in me and our steering group, this time, than in the naïve supporting cast surrounding him nearly thirty years earlier. His New Deal sensibility and poor Irish background gave him a tenacious belief in what he saw as the promise of America. He spoke of the SP-1 debate as a bad administrative move on the part of the University of California regents, and he felt that it was the result of the brief and ineffective leadership of then UC President Jack Peltason, from 1992 to 1995.

Several independent, intriguing figures filled out our steering group: Ricardo Stanton-Salazar, an untenured Chicano professor from the sociology department; Alma Hill, a recent UCSD student body president who has become a successful teacher and vice principal in one of the toughest middle schools in town; and Dr. Randy Souviney, Bud's right hand in the Teacher Education Program. I hired Andrew Sutherland, our committee's only UCSD student, as my provost's intern and offered him a place on the steering committee in the summer of 1995.

Just as valuable to the campaign as any of the faculty, student, or administrative voices were those of Walter and Maisha Kudumu. Together, they ran one of San Diego's successful parent education organizations. Although their organization constantly muddled along on a shoestring budget, the Kudumus were aging black revolutionaries from the sixties who, somehow, maintained their faith and continued to devote their enormous energy to the cause of social justice. Although I had only invited Walter to serve on the steering committee, the two together functioned as a powerful protest unit. Consequently, Maisha usually attended meetings (without invitation) and could be depended upon to ask the tough questions. She often delivered soulful panegyrics that reminded everyone that we were not just addressing a nameless bureaucracy—we were fighting for the lives of children.

The presence of the Kudumus on the UCSD Charter School Steering Committee was the only issue on which Bill and I disagreed. Although he never stated the point outright, he felt that they were a bit too vulgar to be adequate spokespersons for a highly visible project sponsored by the University of California. My view was that we needed powerful and legitimate voices from the community we wished to serve so our efforts would be trusted by single black mothers and newly arrived immigrant families from Mexico. We had to build coalitions across campus and town.

The steering committee, strong in its diversity and capacities, embodied a type of public university and community partnership of which Gilman might have dreamed in the years following the Civil War. By the summer of 1995, we were ready to push for a vision that long predated the affirmative action dispute then shaking the University of California system to its foundation. The intensely emotional atmosphere generated by that public high stakes debate, however, would lend a new sense of urgency to our project by the end of 1995.

But I, too, had my own personal sense of urgency inextricably interwoven with our project.

The summer of 1995 found me tumbling in grief following the death of my wife of thirty years, from ovarian cancer. I sought to stop my freefall by consuming my waking days with work. As fall approached, I began to put together the initial concrete steps for what was eventually to become the first charter school for poor children on a university campus anywhere in the United States.

On August 8, 1995, I wrote to the UCSD Charter School Steering Committee to set out our charge and to explain my position. We had, by that point, chatted informally for two years about the idea of opening a charter school under the aegis of the University of California. Bud had collected data about innovative schools around the country. Each of us had read widely and talked with leading educators from across the nation to find out what worked and what did not. "The lead-up to the regental fray on July 20th," I wrote, referring to the highly-charged discussion of SP-1, "convinced me that UCSD, for its own future, must play a more direct interventionist role on behalf of underrepresented student populations *before* we go out to recruit them." Beyond affirmative action policies, I argued, our university had to come to terms with its own failures and its own responsibility in responding directly to the needs of its immediate community:

> Judging solely by the spotty data available, as well as credible anecdotal evidence, the outreach efforts at most UC campuses are ineffective. The preparatory programs the University of California depends upon to reach disadvantaged populations—Early Academic Outreach Program (EAOP), Summer Bridge, Student Outreach, Admissions, & Recruitment (SOAR), UNEX-sponsored summer teacher training, Upward Bound, Student Opportunity and Access Program (SOAP), Transfer Articulation Agreement, and even Partners-At-Learning, and many others—are, at best, either too late in a student's intellectual development to be effective, too passive, or too isolated and completely uncoordinated with other outreach efforts to make a substantive difference in the acquisition of skills or in the development of a higher order of thinking in the targeted student population.
> —Cecil Lytle, August 8, 1995 memo

The Idea

Over the next few months, we distilled the past two years of research on the underperformance of low-income African American and Mexican American children in California's public schools. Although both groups together formed more than fifty percent of public school enrollments, these groups represented less than ten percent of the University of California's student registrants. We felt that a well-conceived and well-run university charter school for these underrepresented groups would offer significant and needed competition for the failing schools found throughout the inner cities. Further, it was our belief that such a school would appropriate the educational values and techniques of the university campus and offer a coherent model of the best teaching and learning practices. The goal was to enable its students to walk through the front door of the most selective universities and colleges. To develop a proposal for a university-based charter school, we organized ourselves into smaller workgroups to pull information together and craft the initial contours of a proposal.

Our target populations were African American and Mexican American children who languished in unimaginative and overwhelmed local public schools, and who were historically absent from the University of California's entering classes. Our objective was to build a college-preparatory secondary school that would recruit underrepresented black and brown children, and that would serve as a model for quality education for inner-city schools. But we knew such a direct approach would not withstand regental scrutiny now that SP-1 forbade the use of racial background in UC admissions.

While writing the proposal, therefore, we had to talk out of both sides of our mouths. Much of the document spoke of serving underrepresented low-income students. Without explicitly saying so, everyone knew that meant African American, Latino (i.e. chiefly Mexican American), and Native American students. Preliminary studies showed that if we set the admission criteria to serve low-income students in San Diego County, we would scoop up an ample percentage of the black and brown students typically, abundantly, and unfortunately found among the poorer communities of the urban area.

The proposal went to great lengths to tacitly associate underrepresentation with low-income and minority populations. All available census data confirmed our loose dialectical approximations and conclusions. But it was still a risky gambit, and we were not certain that detractors would overlook our vague language; especially since they knew I had opposed UC Regent Ward Connerly's anti-affirmative action efforts earlier that year. The admissions policy spelled out in the proposal had to circumnavigate a political maelstrom and rely on healthy doses of Republican guilt and Democratic contrition.

Early on, we thought to create a UCSD charter school in San Diego's inner city. However, we abandoned the idea in preference to establishing the school on the campus, due to a multitude of obstructions placed in our path by the local school district, labor unions, and civic groups. It had become clear as early as 1994 that we would have to build the charter school on campus if the university were to maintain control of it.

The basic requirements for outlining and gaining approval for a charter school seemed straightforward. Charter legislation provided opportunities for teachers, parents, students, and other members of the community to establish and maintain schools which could operate independently from the existing school district structure. We designed our petition to meet the requirements of California's 1992 Charter School Act:

> Improve all student learning with special emphasis on expanding experiences for pupils who are identified as academically low-achieving; encourage the use of different and innovative teaching methods; create professional opportunities for teachers; provide parents and pupils with expanded choices in the types of educational venues available to them; and, to hold the schools established under this provision accountable for student outcomes.
>
> —Proposal to Establish the UCSD Charter High School, Fall of 1996

Within thirty days of receiving a proposal, the legislation required the local school district to hold a public hearing on the provisions of the charter, at which time the board should consider the level of employee and parental support for the petition. Further, a charter school "shall not be sectarian in its programs, admissions policies, employment practices, and all other operations." Because a charter school remained the legal entity of the sponsoring district, we could not and would not charge tuition. Upon approval by the district, our charter school would receive from the district all funds applicable to serving the same students at their inventory schools. Because we were targeting low-income students, we anticipated receiving additional local and federal funds usually aimed at students requiring special or categorical instructional support.

All UCSD Charter High School student applicants would be low-income as described by the federal Free/Reduced Lunch Program. That meant that a family of four, for instance, could not earn more than 150% of the poverty level or no more than $19,000 annually. Secondly, the students must be the first in their family to attend and graduate from a four-year college or university. More specifically, neither the parent nor guardian could hold a four-year college degree.

We wanted to reach the families in most need of the school, and this second provision proved an important bulwark against clever manipulations by overly aggressive, wealthier parents. When rumors about our project started to circulate, for instance, I received a letter and then a telephone call from a La Jolla divorcée who inquired about the admission criteria for the new UCSD high school. Upon learning that the proposed school would be exclusively for low-income children, she argued that since she was recently divorced (and temporarily living in expectation of a large alimony settlement from her adulterous, rich husband), she was, at that moment, without income. Although she and her children lived in a multi-million dollar La Jolla home, she wanted them to have access to any secondary school run by UCSD. I took comfort in the fact that, despite the elimination of affirmative action, the highly educated and wealthy were not yet a protected class (legally speaking).

The third, and perhaps most ambiguous criterion asked that both the youngster and the family display the proper motivation for attending a college preparatory secondary school. Here, we sought indicators of student and family dedication to the educational enterprise, such as a proven record of regular school attendance, completion of homework assignments, and a letter of recommendation from both a current teacher and a person from their community. Our school, after all, hoped to demonstrate what underrepresented, public school students could achieve when their families and the larger community worked together.

Finally, to strengthen the research possibilities of the project, we determined early on to admit students by lottery once they met the qualifying criteria. This admissions procedure would insure that we were inoculated against the accusation of skimming or "cherry-picking" only the best kids. The procedure also guaranteed that there would be a cohort group of similarly profiled students for longitudinal comparison.

We planned to build a small school of 240 students, equally divided among grades nine through twelve. All of the research on education proved that youngsters from low-income backgrounds enter the upper grades far behind their grade-level in reading, mathematics, and just about every other subject. The budgetary plan for the school called for subsidizing a student-to-teacher ratio of fifteen-to-one so that students would receive as much attention as necessary to catch up. Rafael Hernandez, moreover, contributed an elegant description of how university students would receive service-learning academic credit for tutoring in the charter school.

In terms of the hard realities of finances and real estate, the steering committee's proposal called upon UCSD to provide acreage on the west side of the campus, amid all of the university classrooms and administrative buildings. This became one of the early points of contention. The California Charter School Act of 1992 provided that the Average Daily Attendance (ADA) funds attached to each student in his or her local school district would follow the student to the new institution and so subsidize the basic operating expenses of the charter school. The university would have to raise the capital resources for a new building and provide land on campus upon which to build it.

While UCSD's Academic Senate bickered, Andrew Sutherland, my undergraduate student intern, successfully put together a $50,000 grant application to the California Department of Education for charter school planning money. The grant allowed Bud to host weekly meetings with a dozen local school teachers to develop the academic structure of our proposed school. The meetings were held in the evenings and proved both enlightening and frustrating. What was clear, however, was that all of the recommended innovations were widely known in the literature of school reform and fully agreed upon by the teachers we had gathered. What these discussions demonstrated was that public schools were prohibited, by a variety of collective bargaining agreements and district policies, from implementing a coherent and full regimen of reforms that would support a high-expectations environment within a school.

Even as we prepared to formally submit the proposal to establish a UCSD Charter High School to the San Diego Board of Education, I went to see officials in the San Diego Teachers' Association. Friends who taught in the San Diego public schools had warned that the teachers' union had decided to continue their anti-charter school stance and to sabotage our effort. Following Pat Ledden's advice, Andrew sent ahead copies of our most recent proposal draft in preparation for the late afternoon meeting.

While I waited for the union reps to arrive at the dingy café we agreed upon, I suddenly felt like I was in a scene out of *The Godfather*. We were to gather to break bread and reach an accord, and I was to give them an offer they would likely refuse.

The meeting was tense, but its outcome was certain, at least, in my mind. A distillation of their complaints centered on our refusal to accept the collective bargaining agreement into our charter. The enabling legislation didn't require adoption of local contract agreements and it was our sense that inviting the union into the planning and policy of the school meant losing all of our control over decisions governing the charter. Although the representatives swore that we could work things out, I was just as determined not to abdicate responsibility for the shape of the charter school to the local teachers' association as I was to give over its control to the UCSD faculty.

Their fallback position was to demand representation on the board of directors of the UCSD Charter High School. I said no, as politely as I could. Although we departed amicably, it was clear that they were not done with their attempts to thwart the establishment of a charter school on the UC San Diego campus, or anywhere else.

Their position was problematic only to the extent that it contradicted what their rank and file teachers were telling us confidentially. The union was in the same delicate spot, therefore, as the university's faculty—approval of the UCSD Charter High School undermined their authority, but because of its populist nature they could not be seen publicly opposing the idea. The UCSD faculty committees, on the other hand, would have a direct vote on the school's future and had to be handled with a curious mixture of dexterity and firmness, although it was never clear to me how accurately the committees actually represented wider faculty opinion. It is reasonable to assume that most of the faculty members were too busy to really care, as long as the project didn't cost them anything. For the vast majority of the UCSD faculty, the charter school was, most likely, off the radar screen.

The Argument Ensues

By late 1995, word was leaking out about our attempts to draft a proposal for a charter school. Like a family secret making the rounds at a cocktail party, most comments were far off the mark. Bud Mehan heard from a highly misinformed secondary school teacher in the community that we were planning to open a school for children of parents with AIDS, a neighbor congratulated me one morning for our plan to establish an academy for the deaf, and a campus colleague told Pat Ledden that he did not think it was such a good idea for us to be championing a school for ex-felons. Clearly, we needed to set the record straight on just what we were considering before the mounting rumors overtook and sabotaged our effort. If the faculty defined the project for itself, through innuendo, the school would surely die before the proposal was even announced. We decided to hold a series of open meetings on campus to present our plan. Although advertised through traditional faculty channels, the meetings were poorly attended.

Our friends came by and lent their encouragement, but the faculty who had privately expressed opposition did not come to speak or listen.

At first, those sedate public forums lulled us into thinking that the absence of a willing opposition meant that there was no opposition. But after being accosted several times in the parking lots and hallways of the campus, we realized that opposition had indeed begun to gather, albeit surreptitiously. With our draft proposal circulating through faculty back channels, it soon became the topic of many conversations on campus. No one, however, spoke openly against the idea. Apparently, the faculty whispering against our proposal found it difficult to publicly declare their unwillingness to share the campus with poor children.

For the last of the informal open meetings in 1995, we decided to stage a mock debate in an attempt to draw out spokespersons for the opposition. From encounters at the Faculty Club salad bar, we knew the criticisms well. So, we developed a series of questions we would ask each other at the meeting. We tested the strategy on Bill and, with a twinkle in his eye, he approved it.

At the final meeting, we recognized some of those we knew to be opponents of the initiative sitting in the very last row of seats. We gave our well-rehearsed, half-hour presentation of the proposal for the thirty or so in attendance, acutely aware of our sullen opponents, before entering the mock-debate segment with some trepidation.

Just as Bud was supposed to ask the first of the planned provocative questions, Bill McGill walked in the back door and sat right next to one of our surprised opponents. Before Bud could begin, Bill raised his hand and asked about the budget for the operation. I had briefly outlined this matter earlier, but the question now presented me with the opportunity to go into more detail; details we had rehearsed the day before in front of Bill.
Bill's neighbor began to squirm.

On cue, I then asked Bud about the research on school reform. He answered smartly while Bill whispered something to another secret antagonist. The chair of the Committee on Educational Policy flinched in response to whatever Bill was saying, while I turned to query Rafael about how university students would be integrated into the charter school's method of instruction. Bill answered that question himself from the back, and then turned to hunch his neighbor while loudly asking, "What do you think?" Our nervous antagonist nodded and said something about the school being an interesting idea. Then she expressed a more general anxiety before abruptly getting up and leaving the room. As she left, Bud wished her speedy recovery from the stabbing cough that had continually punctuated the meeting.

We returned to my office to debrief over a glass of wine. "What the *hell* was that?" Bud asked with a grin as we settled into the sofa and chairs.

"That was triangulation at its best." Rafael replied.

"It was a surprise," I said. "Bill, you didn't follow the rules of engagement. It was wonderful!"

Throughout our jubilant flutter, Bill's eyes twinkled again and again. Finally, twirling his Merlot, he tempered the ruckus by reminding us that we had not been in a real fight yet. It was coming, he warned, but it would most likely take place behind closed doors. His view was that the faculty was disturbed by the idea of sharing the campus with poor kids in general, and that it would justify its fear with the argument that such an effort was not in our mission as a public research university. He seemed happy that his young warriors were smart enough to anticipate and draw out the opposition, but he was obviously worried about the struggle ahead.

This was unlike the Third College debates of the late 1960s. Then, the issue of inclusion was sharply defined as a matter of choosing between the two competing virtues of academic excellence and social responsibility. Establishing a college preparatory charter school on campus for historically underrepresented students, we believed, would derail the old debate between meritocracy and UC outreach. Our project would sidestep the argument over affirmative action by putting forward an idea aimed squarely at academic excellence.

However, Bill persuasively argued that the faculty would take the matter underground because their real fears and prejudices could not be voiced so easily in the light of day. We knew this project served, simultaneously, all three of the university's stated missions—teaching, research, and service. Although we had stymied the opposition temporarily, our sage warned that things were likely to get more difficult. He told us we needed to be diligent, cunning, and benevolently ruthless in the coming weeks and months.

I think Bill was proud of us for doing well that evening. But he had seen it all before, and he knew that some gut-wrenching pain still lay ahead. He tutored us a little more in the art of handling hostile questions, then left. Everyone departed my office with mixed feelings of elation and dread brought on by Bill's carefully tempered optimism. I sat down at the Bösendorfer piano in my office to play some wintry Scriabin preludes, but soon drifted to that other keyboard in my office that had come to dominate more and more of my life.

During the period of the UCSD open meetings on the charter school proposal, UC President Jack Peltason was struggling to aid the UC Academic Senate's attempt to regain the initiative by establishing a system-wide committee to review UC admissions policy in light of SP-1. He appointed the President's Task Force on Undergraduate Admissions Criteria to recommend ideas for how the University of California's admissions policy could comply with SP-1 and to try to salvage the prerogatives of the faculty in the running of the university. Jack's eventual call letter wisely cast the regents' July mandate as a recommendation from the board of regents to the faculty and administration of the university. He probably hoped the task force, as an administrative instrument, would blunt or divert the highly specific intent of the regents to destroy every vestige of affirmative action. The UC regents, however, saw it otherwise.

The task force was chaired by Arnie Leiman, a congenial and distinguished Berkeley sociologist whose folksy demeanor reminded me very much of Bill McGill. Although the end-run around the regents' anti-affirmative action policy did not work, the data derived by the task force proved, "...the overall effect of eliminating racial and ethnic criteria in admissions across the university as a whole would be a decline of approximately 27%–33% in the number of underrepresented freshmen *admits,* and a decrease of approximately 26%–46% in the number of underrepresented freshman *registrants,* i.e., freshman admits projected ultimately to enroll at UC." Even worse scenarios would come true in 1997 when African American admits to the University of California decreased by 50%.

At about the same time Peltason's task force was at work, important changes had taken place on the San Diego campus. Chemistry Professor Marjorie Caserio had been number two on the campus organization chart until Dick Atkinson left UCSD to become the seventeenth president of the University of California on October 1, 1995. She became the interim chancellor until a permanent successor could be chosen. It was made clear from the start that she did not want the job permanently and wanted her interim status emphasized at every opportunity. In fact, she demanded early on that she be officially referred to as interim chancellor to discourage any hint that she might indeed be in charge. Consequently, we had little expectation that she would either endorse or retard the progress of our proposal.

Immediately following her appointment as interim chancellor, she put out an all-campus bulletin introducing herself. Except for a diversity-related homily to "standards" and "excellence" in the first paragraph, the entire letter was devoted to the regents' anti-affirmative action ruling five months earlier and the need to revise admissions policy regarding the use of race, ethnicity, and gender. The document also signaled the escalation in importance of the campus' Admissions Committee. This was a remarkable development, considering the varied operations, departments, schools, and institutes that usually take up the attention of campus leadership. Clearly, she understood the moment, but felt that she was not in a position to take any strong action, one way or the other, with regard to minority admissions at UCSD. Although liberal lamentations permeate the letter, as a document it is no less remarkable for the amount of attention it focuses solely on affirmative action while assiduously avoiding the term itself.

Understandably, we were not quite sure of her motivation when she called for a meeting with the UCSD Charter School Steering Committee. It was clear, however, that the non-faculty bureaucrats surrounding her wanted to kill the project. It would mean new work for them, and they correctly perceived that a charter school for poor secondary school students on the UCSD campus was not something the faculty would easily endorse. University bureaucrats seem to have a knack for sniffing out faculty opinion and murdering in their infancy those initiatives that might grow up to be trouble.

With some suspicion, then, the members of the steering committee quickly collated the data for the meeting with Caserio. Andrew Sutherland and I repeatedly stayed in the office long after nightfall, finalizing the draft proposal and fretting over every syllable of the executive summary we would give to her along with the full draft proposal.

Nevertheless, we also considered the possibility that the meeting might be an auspicious one. Caserio had it in her power, after all, to jumpstart the project and offer the first positive, feasible plan for a new era in University of California outreach. Such a move would put UCSD out in front of the other campuses on the single issue of most concern to the system as a whole, and it would serve as a sign of UCSD's goodwill in a troubling time. Perhaps Bill was thinking along these lines as our little group made its way to Caserio's office the morning of the meeting. Somewhere on the path between the Geisel Library and a picturesque eucalyptus grove, he put a fatherly hand on Andrew's shoulder. "If this school were offered as a solution thirty years ago," he said, "the campus would have jumped at the chance."

The steering committee gathered in the office of the interim chancellor on Monday, January 22, 1996 to describe the basic tenets of the draft proposal for a UCSD charter school. Marjorie presented herself as an honest broker, well meaning, but decidedly indecisive. Following an earlier practice of Joe Watson's, I had sent ahead copies of our draft and brought with me copies of the summary we had prepared. In attendance were most of the university's high-ranking civil servant class of vice chancellors, a few academics, and the steering committee. I wanted to dispel all of the strange rumors floating around the campus and city about our project and give a coherent presentation of the charter school and how we intended to proceed.

The room was already full of bureaucrats when we arrived. Chancellor Atkinson always had a good sense that bookkeepers and lawyer-like administrators were essential in running a complex billion-dollar corporation like UCSD. Further, he intuitively understood that lawyers and accountants should be on tap, not on top. Even while listening to their advice, he knew that they were not necessarily informed by the urgent and irregular passions of the academic community. Their bottom lines, that is to say, needed to be in the service of the occasionally improbable visions of the university faculty. Now, with his ascendancy to the UC president's office, there was a power vacuum at UCSD that the civil servants were more than willing to fill.

Although we congenially quipped and joked as we took our seats and the meeting gradually came to order, it was clear that the bureaucrats had just met with Marjorie to dissuade her from taking any favorable action on our behalf. Marjorie began by saying, with obvious irritation, that she had no intention of approving this or any other such proposal without scrutiny by the UCSD Academic Senate. Everyone around the room tensed. The message could not have been clearer.

The UCSD Academic Senate had never concerned itself with outreach programs. Indeed, none of its numerous standing committees oversaw campus outreach. When Caserio relegated this matter to the academic senate, she gave it an ill-disguised death sentence. Atkinson had scrupulously avoided the academic senate whenever he truly wanted to get something done. Consulting the UCSD Academic Senate was an annoying afterthought for him once the major pieces of whichever entrepreneurial puzzle he desired were in place.

Anyone aware of the capability of a college professor to perform verbal gymnastics when faced with even the most direct question would also understand why we knew instantly that sending our draft proposal to the senate without the chancellor's endorsement or comment—where dozens and dozens of tenured professors strewn within a labyrinth of committees would discuss it *ad nauseum*—was a means to strangle the project.

After preemptively announcing our fate, however, she asked that we tell her about the draft proposal. I recovered as quickly as I could and handed out copies of the summary report before beginning a ten-minute description so well rehearsed that it flowed with a familiar ease. Since the attendees had received the draft proposal the previous week, I stressed the major points such as the eligibility criteria for selecting students. Then I reviewed the California charter school legislation soliciting "an entity to develop a proposal for how they would develop and run a charter school." I was careful to point out that, if approved, the operating budget for the school would be provided by the San Diego Unified School District, using the Average Daily Attendance funds attached to the 240 students.

Towards the end of my short presentation, Pat Ledden chimed in with words of reinforcement on the matter of proposed student eligibility. I asked Bud to briefly describe his research in the area that confirmed our assumptions regarding student achievement. When we finished, the assembly seemed even more irritated at the proposal's concreteness and reiterated the declaration that we needed faculty senate approval before entertaining such a risky venture.

I countered to say that the senate had never exercised authority over campus outreach initiatives, and that my work on the UC Outreach Task Force led me to report that the campus would soon be receiving large sums of new UC-outreach funds to counteract the anticipated deleterious effects of SP-1.

The campus accountants confirmed the "interim" nature of the chancellor's office and, once again, recited the need for senate oversight in this matter. I thought they might gag with glee. They knew the senate well and had certainly heard the backroom chatter against our effort. They knew, furthermore, that they could feed the academic senate dire predictions of terrible financial consequences brought on by a UCSD charter school. A year later, the faculty senate would be in full gallop opposing the project, and the non-academic civil servants in the room would be the architects of the opposition.

Bill's presence added stature and credibility to our effort. He was a senior campus guru who had seen his share of difficult enterprises and knew faculty angst well. His presence lent the occasion and the project an invaluable dignity. Rafael and I were the protagonists arguing on behalf of an edgy proposal. Andrew, our undergraduate, could play the angry young man when the time came, and no one would fault him for it. Pat Ledden, however, was the campus diplomat; he was able to speak easily with foes who would not otherwise give me the time of day. Known across the campus as a patrician Irishman whose intellect was rivaled only by his charm, Pat, the elder statesman, could be counted on to smooth our affairs whenever debate got out of hand. He sat across from me, next to Andrew, and I nervously hoped he could keep our youngest representative from making any embarrassing outbursts.

Although tense, the meeting might have ended cordially if Marjorie had not chastised the steering committee. She lectured us about acting precipitously, reprimanding us for holding our open meetings across the campus. Andrew bristled. Pat Ledden came unglued.

"No, Marjorie! No! You say you can't move without the faculty being consulted, and then you criticize us for providing the faculty with information about the proposal. We've given the faculty every opportunity to review and be informed about what we're doing," Pat said, tearing off his thick-rimmed eyeglasses and looking her sternly in the eye. "Now you have to decide. You want to send this back to the faculty so that you won't have to act, but the faculty has studied the problem, we've been studying it, and now we must act! We must act!" He tossed the glasses aimlessly across the huge rectangular conference table and rapped his knuckles on the table, punctuating each of his "we must act" statements with a sharp "crack-crack."

Bill put a firm hand on Pat's glasses-tossing arm. "What Pat means to say is that we're prepared to finish the proposal and seek review by senate committees. Do you have a recommendation which committees we should consult?" he asked gently.

The question caught them off guard. They probably had envisioned the UCSD Academic Senate as some sort of featureless black hole into which we would descend, never to be heard from again. Someone on the other side of the table convulsively blurted out, "All of them." We agreed to follow the interim chancellor's advice and exited the room as genially as we could.

Pat's face finally returned to its normal color as we crossed in front of the library. He hated dishonesty and hypocrisy. I was amused and surprised since Pat was serving on the steering committee because of his endearing and calming demeanor. We headed in near-silence to a little café to debrief. As we sat down, I kidded him, "Now that you've replaced me as the warrior, Pat, you've left me the role of peacekeeper. I don't know if I can do it."

We laughed at the reversal of fortunes and our ambidexterity as a committee. Pat's fury came just as I was about to tell the chancellor and the others about the successful meeting I had the week before with some major donors about funding the project. Had Pat not interrupted, it might have been Marjorie flinging her glasses instead at the thought that I was already out raising money for the charter school.

Dr. Patrick J. Ledden
Photo courtesy of University Communications
and Public Affairs at UC San Diego

Chapter Three

Death by a Thousand Committees

For several months before and after the meeting with Interim Chancellor Caserio, Bud and I had been in correspondence or meeting with subcommittees of the UCSD Academic Senate. In the University of California system, faculty representatives in each campus' senate enjoy broad legislative powers and vote to advise their respective chancellors in the most serious matters. While laudable, such a democratic system is at risk of suffering the same abuses to which national political systems are vulnerable. A democratic body, perversely, can provide the perfect cover should the desire arise among its leadership to stifle a progressive idea while preserving the virtuous image of a public institution in service to its people. If our perceptions were right, our nascent charter school was about to be strangled in its cradle and in the dark. No group, perhaps, can throttle the life out of an initiative with more gusto than tenured professors sitting in relative obscurity on academic committees while getting high on coffee.

The Proposal

We had sent the various committees making up the academic senate leadership what we were calling a "draft proposal" of the charter school in order to draw their fire and comments early on. The cover letter mentioned that we wanted to have their opinions on the fledgling proposal before we came back with an official document.

The text of the proposal ran thirty-one pages with an equal number of pages of charts, graphs, and tables to back up our initiative with hard data. Feeling plucky, I inscribed on the front cover a quotation from the speech Marian Wright Edelman, president of the Children's Defense Fund, delivered at the dedication ceremony marking Third College's name change to Thurgood Marshall College in 1993. Edelman remarked that Thurgood Marshall didn't just witness change, "he created it." It was my view that a public university, too, existed to be an agent of change and that there was no better mission than to make change happen for the least privileged. Bill warned me that foregrounding Edelman's electric rhetoric would unnecessarily inflame some faculty members who were to pass judgment on the proposal in the senate. But I could not resist my own need to strike at least one blow for progressivism before receiving the pummeling I knew was coming.

We had prepared the three main sections of the proposal in as straightforward a manner as possible: 1) "Introduction: The Problem and a Proposed Solution;" 2) "Mission Statement and Goals;" and, 3) "Provisions of the Charter High School."

Bud was responsible for the language contained in the first section. There, he laid out an examination of the research literature regarding secondary school preparation for UC admission by class and race. Although the conclusions were obvious, the quantitative analysis was an excoriating condemnation of the academic preparation available to youngsters from low-income populations in San Diego County and nationwide:

> Students from historically disenfranchised groups do poorly in school by comparison with their well-to-do contemporaries. They drop out at a higher rate. They score lower on standardized tests. Their grades are lower. And more importantly for the topic of this proposal, the creation of a college preparatory high school on the UCSD campus, they do not attend college as often.
>
> These same students are expected to compose an increasing percentage of the United States population through the early years of the 21st century (Pelavin & Kane, 1990; Carter

& Wilson, 1991).

...The problem of underrepresentation is evident at the University of California. Students from low-income African American and Latino backgrounds are underrepresented in our classrooms.... The continued absence of historically disenfranchised populations from the University of California means that there will be fewer African American doctors and scientists, fewer lawyers and teachers whose ancestry is rooted in the Mexican American communities of California.

Continuing uninterrupted, this pattern will produce an Apartheid condition within California in which the numerically largest cultural populations are governed, taught, and administered by an ever-shrinking minority elite.

While true and roundly supported by the scholarly data, this subversive language harkened back twenty-five years to the Lumumba-Zapata Demands. Furthermore, our introduction pointed out the failure of Kerr's Master Plan as an inter-segmental educational device to advance the education of children often left out of higher education. Kerr had envisioned a connected scheme of community colleges and state universities that would allow students of differing abilities to eventually gain access to the University of California. What evolved, however, was a three-tiered set of cul-de-sacs wherein the poor secondary school preparation of low-income students was not sufficient to allow these students to advance through the system and achieve a UC degree.

Also underlying the effort was our belief that a particular social and educational advantage could be attributed to the highly theoretical training offered by the University of California, resulting in an intellectual perspective that naturally led students to pursue advanced and professional degrees. These graduates would become the executives, the bankers, the lawyers, and the leaders of a modern and diverse California of the near future. The mission of UC outreach, therefore, required that historically disenfranchised populations must become not only eligible for the least rigorous state schools, but also competitively eligible for the most selective and prestigious of the UC campuses, professional schools, and graduate schools.

Our proposed solution was, in fact, a challenge to all existing UC outreach programs. The many outreach efforts in play for the past thirty years were not engaging or intensive enough to help students become competitively eligible for the elite Berkeley, Los Angeles, and San Diego campuses. It was not surprising when the directors of those UC outreach programs proved to be among our bitterest enemies. These programs simply could not adequately prepare low-income or minority youngsters for admission to the selective UC campuses. The UCSD Charter High School that we proposed was not only a threat to the elite culture of the campus, but a threat to the affirmative action industry that had failed the university and the populations in need.

We pegged our approach to the model of other UC initiatives designed to encourage wholesale economic development and social tranquility. Bud introduced the idea of copying the success of UC's Agricultural Field Station model. He described our ambitious proposal for an on-campus charter school for poor children as the educational analog to the monumentally successful UC Agricultural Field Station. Our urban Educational Field Station would be copied by most school districts, we believed, and lead to widespread educational reform.

From the beginning, we chose to view the UCSD Charter High School as both an experiment and a national demonstration project. It would not be competition to local public schools in the sense championed by conservative politicians promoting voucher schools. Rather, our model would serve as an inspiration for both the public and private sectors. Our effort was to be aimed at disadvantaged youngsters whose educational advancement would be accelerated so that they would perform at an academic level consistent with their more advantaged counterparts. The school would not only demand and expect high standards, but also provide highly specialized resources supporting the core areas of reading, writing, and mathematics. In a spirit contrary to the No Child Left Behind initiative, we wanted to demonstrate the positive effects of allocating resources to disadvantaged students rather than taking money away to punish a failing school.

Bud's research informed our proposal and challenged prevailing American educational policy. "The principles of the UCSD Charter High School are derived from current thinking about cognitive development and the social organization of schooling," he wrote. "The idea of providing one academically rigorous form of curriculum and instruction to all students, accompanied by a system of social and academic supports," he said, "is better understood if placed against the background of the history of educational policy in the United States."

He specifically addressed "tracking," a standard practice in American K-12 public education, where students are separated into different ability groups early in their careers. Condemning tracking as an historical aberration and insufficient for the technological future of the twenty-first century, Bud went on to describe its history and our aversion to this practice:

> …Educators in the United States have responded to differences among individuals and groups by separating students and altering the content of the curriculum to which they are exposed. Since the 1920's, most high schools have offered a 'tracked' curriculum—sequences of academic classes that range from slow-paced remedial courses to rigorous ones.

In other words, ability grouping begun informally in elementary school becomes institutionalized by middle school and further entrenched in high school. The curriculum for youngsters designated as "underperforming" is reduced in scope, content, and pace relative to that offered to "high-ability" groups. Students who have been assigned to the "college prep" track receive a distinct curriculum and are separated from students who have been assigned to the "vocational track." It is a pernicious system that can earmark youngsters for failure before they reach the ninth grade.

> Tracking rests on the assumptions about the nature of the occupational structure and the role of schooling in an industrial society. Tracking was justified at the height of industrializa-

tion because it supported a long-standing belief in the United States and Great Britain that a crucial function of schools is to prepare students for jobs (Davis & Moore, 1945.) The industrial revolution divided labor into jobs and occupations that require different kinds of skills. As a result, workers who have different kinds of knowledge were needed to fill those different kinds of jobs. The function of schools was to serve as a rational sorting device, matching students' talents to the demands of the workplace (Turner, 1960). Thus, rigorous academic classes could prepare students heading for jobs that require college degrees, whereas vocational programs could prepare students for less skilled jobs or for technical training after high school.

Tracking students for different work lives, he argued, was thought fair because students were believed to possess fixed intellectual abilities, motivations, and aspirations while different jobs demanded different skills and talents: "Thus, a tracked curriculum with its ability-grouped classes was viewed as both functional and democratic."

Our proposal, on the other hand, embraced the universal development theory that asserts a different conception of human capacity and school organization and avoids the consequences of negative labeling associated with low expectations. Our teachers and curriculum would place all of the UCSD Charter High School students in rigorous college preparatory classes. We would adopt the proposition that tracking is decidedly undemocratic and sabotages the potential of students and families historically underrepresented at the University of California. In Section Two, under the words "Mission Statement," our draft proposal said:

> The UCSD Charter High School is conceived to provide an intensive college preparatory educational environment for low-income and other historically underrepresented student populations at the University of California.
>
> Through the application of tutor-assisted teaching, the goal is to create a highly enriched four-year instructional scheme

that will prepare the graduates to distinguish themselves in assessment, evaluation, and standardized tests that will make them competitively eligible at the University of California or any other selective institution of higher learning.

Section Three, "Provisions of the Charter School," discussed eligibility criteria, recruitment techniques, the application process, curriculum, class size, teacher qualifications, assessment, and governance in detail. While this might seem to be the more quotidian part of the proposal, in reality it gave it teeth. Just as Angela Davis and Herbert Marcuse's revolutionary statements finally took form in the real brick-and-mortar institution called Third College, our ideas needed to assume a tangible form with definable features, if they were to have an impact in the world. The proposal's final section was the blueprint for that form.

Dr. Hugh "Bud" Mehan

The first five months of 1997 were extremely busy with preparations for several faculty meetings each week and many tinkering revisions of the draft proposal to satisfy the whims of key committee chairs, who continued to hold the entire project hostage in their senate committees.

One of our first meetings was to take place February 7th with the Planning and Budget Committee. However, two days before we were to gather face-to-face, the chair of that committee sent around a blistering criticism of the draft. Rather than wait to ask questions or allow us to fully explain our plans in person, the chairman took a first shot at the draft proposal, which he knew would have a chilling effect at the meeting. His five-page memo specifically attacked the eligibility criteria for admission to the UCSD Charter High School—criteria we had yet to discuss with his committee.

The dissemination of misinformation proved to be a key tactic of the reactionary opponents of the charter school initiative in the faculty senate. Colleagues sitting on the gauntlet of committees that the interim chancellor had asked us to traverse seemed ready to circulate distorted or inaccurate ideas before we even had a chance to meet and examine the facts of the proposal together. We expected some opposition at the meeting with the Planning and Budget Committee. We were caught off-guard, admittedly, by the rapidity of this first attack from its chair.

The letter was addressed to the chair of the UCSD Academic Senate and copied to nearly everyone on campus. I was furious at what I perceived to be the sneaky nature of an ambush tactic. Here was a preemptive strike at the project, based on an opposing logic that, it seemed to me, desperately needed ignorance for its credibility. While the draft document spelled out the admissions criteria in detail, and while the proposal emphasized that low-income children were the target of our effort, the memo equivocated over likely yield rates as compared to La Jolla High School—the best school in the county and one attended by children from some of San Diego's wealthiest families, as well as children of the UCSD faculty.

After we finally met with the Planning and Budget Committee two days later, I wrote the members a letter summarizing both the meeting and the February 5th letter of ambush. Bud wisely discarded my inflammatory first draft, as it was the classic angry letter that should never be sent. In its place, he helped to craft a four-page retort that went through the memo line by line, correcting errors of fact and highlighting points on which we all agreed during the February 7th meeting.

This exercise in patience proved a precursor for successive battles with the other senate committees.

The chair of Planning and Budget and the other committee chairs sought to associate themselves and their committees with the altruistic goals of the charter school proposal but would go on to say, essentially, that there may be other more profitable ideas for the University of California to pursue in its quest for true diversity. No one from Planning and Budget offered a description of what those alternatives might look like, however.

While the academic senate committees sought to drown us in a sea of disparaging memos, convoluted arguments, and tedious verbiage, our steering committee pressed on as if the school actually would become a physical presence on the campus. I was not sure if we were valiantly undaunted or hopelessly optimistic.

The encounters with the other dozen or so committees were just as difficult as the one with Planning and Budget. By Valentine's Day, the steering committee was meeting almost every day in response to the latest criticism or attack. Aside from being an exemplar of what was to come, this first encounter quite accurately predicted a turning of the tables with regards to the classical position of conservatives and progressives. Allegedly liberal tenured faculty members were fighting us in committee, and I wondered if their conservative adversaries would support us for equally shaky reasons.

Strange Bedfellows

A few months later, Bill McGill received a two-page letter, signed jointly by two extremely conservative psychology professors, which confirmed for me the strange, political role reversal sensed earlier. The younger of the two men was an outspoken supporter of the anti-affirmative action movement and had traveled the state speaking against racial quotas and preferential treatment in UC admissions. As quantitative psychologists, they took us to task about some of our predictions for the size of the projected graduating class and the number of students who would be competitively eligible for the more selective UC campuses. The central tone of the letter was unequivocally favorable toward the initiative, however. They championed the suggestion of a senior campus political scientist in his call for a lottery in admissions to the charter school. Apparently, none of them had read the lottery description already in our proposal.

I wasn't sure who was using whom. Had I moved closer to the Right by hinting at the dissolution of public education, or were conservatives beginning to support more aggressive targeted outreach? I asked Bill this question a few weeks later and he assured me that more and more people would be finding novel ways to support a good idea. I took his suggestion as a positive development, but worried that our "good idea" would become enmeshed in the tangled battle between the Left and the Right over attempts at social engineering by the university.

A curious routine started to emerge. After each meeting, Bud and I would meet to compare our reactions to the discussion. In every case, we felt that we had swayed a majority of the committee members to our side. However, a week or two later, we would receive an angry or extremely negative letter from the committee chairman. Due to the number of complaints she was receiving, the interim chancellor appointed a campus-wide feasibility committee to vet the proposal.

The January 31, 1996 Feasibility Task Force appointment letter charged the group to report on the following salient charter school issues: "The mission, curriculum, and administration of the charter school; student selection, student social life, and support services; location and facilities; budget projections and revenue sources; liability and insurance; UCSD goals, objectives, and expectations; interactions between the charter school, UCSD, and their respective populations; and evaluation and assessment of student outcomes."

The Feasibility Task Force was asked to report back by March 8th "…or as soon thereafter as possible." The chair of the group was Vice Chancellor Joe Watson. As was his custom, Joe played his cards so close to the vest that it was never clear just where he personally stood on the project. He had remained aloof all during the previous years of planning and discussions and rarely attended either steering committee meetings or our open town meetings on the topic. It was clear that the regents' SP-1 decision and our steering committee's insistence on achieving a competitive eligibility standard for UCSD outreach programs were putting added pressure on Joe and on the outreach programs under his charge.

In fact, Joe had administered himself into a precarious corner. As Third College's provost twenty-five years earlier, he had challenged the chancellor and faculty senate for the survival of the college. But now, totally distanced from those revolutionary instincts, he seemed regrettably stuck in a very high-paying administrative post enforcing the "go slow" wishes of successive chancellors regarding outreach and recruitment of minority students.

On the other hand, Watson, while a reluctant warrior, could still smell the ozone over the battle of ideas and programs in the cause of social justice. He instinctively knew that the UCSD Charter High School was a long shot, but that it was also just the kind of highly visible campus activity that would directly serve a public that UCSD rarely impacts in a positive way. It was hard to envy Joe and the delicate spot he found himself in as we pushed hard against the mounting opposition; campus outreach and recruitment were the responsibility of people who worked for him. He was like a sailboat cast adrift, every push by the steering committee and every reciprocal shove by a recalcitrant faculty senate committee violently rocked his precarious position with an agitating tide that would soon overtake us all.

He and I had more than a few tense encounters in which I questioned his integrity and dedication to what I believed was the natural extension of his efforts to craft Third College so many years earlier when he was its provost.

The feasibility work group's report was delivered almost two months after the March 8 deadline, and the response from the UCSD administration could not have been less happy. In particular, the interim chancellor and the surrounding civil servants were displeased by the clear statement that the UCSD Charter School should be created and ought to: "...be explicitly a unit of UCSD under the direct authority of the chancellor in order to ensure that the full administrative and oversight capabilities of the campus guide the administration of the charter school."

It was thought that the favorable recommendation for the UCSD Charter High School by the Feasibility Task Force would have put the issue to rest and allowed the initiative to go forward, especially since the UCSD Academic Senate spent months carefully selecting faculty members to serve on the committee who could be depended upon to block any remotely favorable outcome. We were wrong. Instead, we were directed to ignore the favorable feasibility report and take the draft charter school proposal to the faculty committees once again.

Just after the favorable report was turned in, Joe and the vice chancellor for academic affairs, Bob Dynes, came to see me in my office. It was an uncommonly cloudy and gloomy morning in La Jolla and my congenitally dark office seemed especially threatening. Their confidential message was that the interim chancellor wanted me to kill the charter school project. In effect, the campus wanted to be seen to be in favor of the project, but to have it silently withdrawn from further consideration by its author. It was their opinion that no one would complain and its disappearance would be welcomed with a sigh of relief by the entire campus.

While withdrawing the proposal might solve their problem, such a sudden gesture on my part, after so much public effort, would undermine my credibility on campus and render me a diffident fool across the state. More plainly put, I was in no mood to slit my own throat without an honest campus debate on the matter, especially in the absence of a better idea. I closed the meeting by saying that I would speak to the interim chancellor in the morning to directly plead the case for the charter school once again. At minimum, I felt that the chancellor's declared "interim-ness" was not a valid position from which to preclude such an enormously important project, in light of the monumental debate that eventually led to SP-1 and the elimination of affirmative action considerations from all UC admissions. She had fallen into the historic UCSD apathy over the underrepresentation of minority students at the UC campuses. It was a regrettable social reality, but most faculty and administrators felt there was little to be done about student diversity other than to state our collective institutional sorrow for the record.

The meeting with the interim chancellor the next morning simultaneously cleared up and further confused the matter. Before I could make my case, the claim was made that it was Joe Watson and Bob Dynes who wanted the charter school killed. It didn't really matter to me who was behind it; I was convinced that all three would have felt more comfortable with the whole matter taken off the table. The trio's behavior modeled the faculty reaction closely. No one wanted to be seen aborting the project, but they all seemed to be clearly interested in an anonymous stillbirth.

In October 1996, the final draft of the Regents' Outreach Task Force Report leaked out, and an old warrior reappeared. Joe Watson wrote a scathing criticism of the report. I gleefully read:

> As a public relations document that will be impressive in the blue and gold colors of the University, the Outreach Task Force Report is well done. However as a guide to a serious understanding of the critical problem of the severe disparities among racial and ethnic groups and strategies to either reduce or eliminate the disparities, the revised report continues to have the major flaws of the first draft.

Knowing that each campus' chancellor had been asked to review the final draft, Joe Watson's stinging rebuttal asked that the newly confirmed UCSD "permanent" chancellor, Bob Dynes, reject the report at the coming meeting of the UC Council of Chancellors. Joe's letter was an endorsement of the Minority Report I had written to the regents in response to the UC Task Force Report. Nevertheless, there was little chance that our opposition to the report would change anything. At least we were now on record warning anyone who would listen about the public relations scam underway.

By the time of the last meeting of the Regents' Outreach Task Force, the African American conservative regent, Ward Connerly, was an already famous, or infamous, celebrity. He usually managed to arrive five to ten minutes after the beginning of each meeting, in order to enter in relative isolation and stride across the length of the room as if he were an anxious prom star under pleasurable review. He rarely took notes or reviewed the minutes of meetings, nor showed any evidence of having tracked the conversation. Rather, he waited for certain buzzwords like "minority," "affirmative action," or "equal rights" to be mentioned; then he would interrupt and launch into one of his well-rehearsed speeches.

We had met several years earlier when I made a public presentation to the UC regents supporting Third College's name change to establish Thurgood Marshall College on the UCSD campus. I sought him out during the private breakfasts and lunch breaks at many regents' meetings in 1993 and 1994. In polite conversation, he was shy and almost tongue-tied while trying to interact. He seemed to have little command of the expanse and totality of the University of California. He seemed to know his role, however, with crystal clarity. He was put on the Board of Regents of the University of California by Governor Pete Wilson solely to wage war on UC affirmative action admissions policies.

Over a stale tuna fish sandwich in the spring of 1994, I first mentioned to him our plan to open a charter school on the San Diego campus. He liked the idea (receiving it in its most narrow conservative interpretation) and went further to say that he supported school vouchers. I told him I did not share his enthusiasm for vouchers but thought that a charter school would allow us to build a model and conduct research in the best practices for educating students who come from historically disenfranchised backgrounds. I also made it clear that I did not share his disdain for affirmative action. To both assertions he said, "Uh huh." I sensed that he was intimidated by my chatting with him up close. Often diverting his eyes, he was reduced to speaking in clipped muttered tones. This was not the image he projected when bellowing in front of television cameras about the sins of "preferential treatment."

The man seated across the tiny table was a mirror image of

the Ward Connerly I had seen on television and in the newspapers. The man nervously chomping on a dill pickle in front of me seemed shy, incompetent, and terrified. It was hard to believe that this was the same man who had out-shouted Jesse Jackson, stood against Al Sharpton, and endured name calling and death threats. Which was the real Ward Connerly?

He promised to support our effort as long as the proposal did not seek to recruit students by race or ethnicity.

On the other end of the political spectrum, Colleen Sabatini was the new president of the UCSD Associated Students and had seen to it that the student body unanimously passed a resolution in support of the UCSD Charter High School. She was only one of a small army of undergraduates who helped save the project. She and Andrew worked non-stop generating support among the student body, holding public rallies, and even staging protests against the obstructionist academic senate committees.

The faculty subcommittees, however, were reluctant to engage in honest debate. Measuring our unwillingness to abandon the project in the face of their opposition, the chair of the campus' academic senate invited me to address a winter 1997 meeting of the UCSD Representative Assembly of the faculty. Taken in the best light, there was the hope that I would be eloquent enough to persuade the faculty to support the effort. Taken at its worst, the gesture was an invitation to attend my own lynching.

Given the slow agenda for the meeting, the drama of the afternoon was planned around my presentation. The chair of the academic senate made perfunctory opening remarks before introducing the new chancellor, Robert Dynes. It was Bob's first meeting with the senate since becoming chancellor a few weeks earlier. The speaker was introduced as a new chancellor who, "…placed a premium on the value of shared governance between the administration and the faculty." That sentiment was echoed in Dynes' comments a few moments later.

The message about the new chancellor couldn't have been clearer. Remarks about shared governance in the chancellor's statement and in the announcement by the senate chair made it abundantly clear that these were well-scripted statements defining and measuring the limits and independence of the new chancellor. Dynes had obviously agreed beforehand to make shared governance a theme of the meeting, and now he had walked into the trap of bargaining away his ability to move unilaterally as chancellor on behalf of issues that mattered to him and to the campus. The focus on shared governance did provide me with a curious sense of relief. Perhaps, I thought desperately, the new chancellor was drawing faculty attention to himself and his leadership and away from the highly controversial charter school proposal and its unrelenting sponsors. At least, that was the hopeful scenario I wanted to believe as I sat awaiting my turn to speak.

The UCSD Charter School Steering Committee made me deliver my remarks several times in rehearsal to ensure I got the facts right. They quizzed me mercilessly to make sure I maintained my cool in the face of challenging questions. Our preparation paid off, although there were no questions. I closed my fifteen-minute address by mentioning that the steering committee was reviewing several possible building sites and that the full proposal could be accessed for review on the Thurgood Marshal College web site. I sat down not knowing if I had won the fight, or even if the real combatants were in the room. The meeting concluded in stony silence and, for me, a rapacious sense of well-being.

The academic senate did not want to be seen as killing this project, but they were being backed into a corner. Except for a few quibbling remarks, the meeting had been cordial. The new chancellor had pledged to do something exciting in response to the negative impositions of SP-1. Our refusal to acquiesce and the constantly growing heat generated by the UC regents' decision to eliminate affirmative action put added pressure on the campus to do "something," but what?

The new chancellor had many times expressed interest in the project privately, although, to my knowledge, he took no active public steps. The academic senate was focusing its attention on the new chancellor—forcing him to decide between an insurgent progressive agenda and a recalcitrant faculty.

Lacking any creative options, the faculty senate resorted to more primal political instincts: they averted their attention away from the issue at hand and focused entirely upon the purely parliamentary procedure of joint governance. If the chancellor favored the idea of the charter school, then they would oppose him on this more courtly governmental issue rather than oppose the charter school proposal directly. The strategy was to force him to take executive action to kill the project or face faculty sanction.

For the past two years, the debate over the establishment of the UCSD Charter High School had essentially gone on between the faculty and the steering committee. What had begun as an internal campus debate was now beginning to take place in full public view. The California press picked up on the story and was cranking up the pressure on the campus with articles unabashedly favorable to the initiative. Throughout the first six months of 1997, the mounting faculty opposition drew scathing criticism from both the California and national press. The UCSD faculty were publicly pilloried for not having the courage of their convictions; the faculty were overwhelmingly in favor of maintaining affirmative action in UC admissions, but did not want a charter school for poor children on their own campus. One notorious cartoon featured a two-panel caricature of a horn-rimmed faculty member holding a protest sign that said, "We Support Affirmative Action." On the other panel, the same bespectacled gentleman showed the reverse of his sign that read, "Charter School: Touch My Research Funds and Die." Daily letters to the editor berated the University of California for hypocritical NIMBY-ism over the charter school. The *Los Angeles Times* called the idea "long overdue." The *San Diego Union-Tribune* published twice-weekly editorials supporting the novel concept.

Ward Connerly and Governor Pete Wilson were peppering their speeches with expressions of open support for an on-campus charter school on the San Diego campus. The notion of a charter school for poor children on campus was no longer merely an academic question, but a very public matter playing out in the national press. The increasing public scrutiny put me in the middle between reticent elements of the faculty and a public howling for a constructive intervention and remedy.

Battle lines had formed in the most peculiar fashion, however. Most progressive liberals on the faculty were either silent or opposed to our effort to open a model charter school. I was troubled by the support of figures like Wilson and Connerly because of their continued opposition to affirmative action. Conservatives were, surprisingly, proving to be our strongest allies.

Andrew Sutherland and I met late one afternoon for cappuccino with representatives of the academic senate. It was their unpleasant task to tell me that the nine draft reports of the senate subcommittees were extremely hostile to the charter school idea. They also indicated that it would be far better for the campus if I simply dropped the entire notion before the subcommittees were forced to kill the project with their fatal assessments. By acquiescing, I could avoid the embarrassment of defeat. My alternatives were either to commit *hara-kiri* or face humiliation. I responded by saying that outreach initiatives had never been the province of the UCSD Academic Senate and that the establishment of our school did not actually require the faculty senate's imprimatur. Further, I argued, it would be to their embarrassment if the project were turned back now, not mine.

Claiming the moral high ground, however, was proving to be expensive. Although I had no interest in becoming the campus martyr, neither was I interested in becoming the senate's victim.

That same week, at a second impromptu meeting with the chair and vice chair of the senate, I reminded my colleagues that defeating the charter school effort did not absolve the senate of its greater responsibility to positively address the widely anticipated negative effects of SP-1. The professors bristled when I said that the senate, "had no new ideas." While true, this tactic did little to dissuade them in their cause to get me to back down. Their threats revealed a misplaced attribution of guilt. They seemed to believe that my intransigence would ultimately lead to a vote of censorship by the faculty senate and removal of the chancellor if Dynes chose to approve the UCSD Charter High School in the face of staunch faculty opposition. Such an outcome was entirely up to the senate, not to me, I wagered. This meeting ended less amicably than the cappuccino-induced civility of a few days earlier. As promised, the nine committee reports were readied for delivery.

Andrew raced over to the Academic Senate Office a few days later to pick up copies after receiving word that they were ready. He knew what having those reports meant. For the past few years, the opposition was largely hidden. Now, all of the intrigue would be gone. For the first time in this long ordeal, the opposition had to take their criticisms beyond closed doors and put them onto paper. Finally, we would have something concrete to fight. My stomach churned at the thought of the conflagration to come.

What would become a public firestorm had heretofore been fought within the courtly parlance of a university campus; from behind masks of civility and polysyllabic words, we had played out the ancient transcendental dance between the "haves" and the "have-nots." The barbarous acts of disregard and abuse perpetrated upon the weak by the powerful had been re-enacted through campus memos, meetings, and e-mail. Now, public figures like the governor and Connerly had gotten involved, and we had official statements from our opponents to which we could respond. I knew I would lose friends in the coming months and that the inevitable gladiatorial spectacle would require someone to die and another to be seen as winning—the stakes were now extremely high and career threatening.

A Thousand Cuts

The committee reports on the UCSD Charter High School proposal were scathing. But their language must be understood in light of typical higher education discourse and gestalt.

For example, the senate committee named the Graduate Council is situated at the heart of the ambitions of a modern research university. It is called a "council" instead of a "committee" to lend itself a greater sense of dignity. "Council" sounds more like a gathering of sages or elders called to oversee the sanctity of graduate education and research, and its members are expected to be more Solomonic than seditious.

The report of the Graduate Council was only three sentences long. Its brevity was an indication of the indirect relationship the council had to the project. Their considerations were most often at the heart of the lofty mission to shepherd new Ph.D. programs offered by academic departments into existence or to escort them off the map, if they failed to aspire to the highest in academic scholarship. Discerning the merits of a charter school for adolescents was, in a way, outside their purview. The Graduate Council's chair, a distinguished anthropologist, led the group to offer its opinion, nonetheless:

> The Graduate Council held a limited discussion of the revised proposal to establish a Charter High School at UCSD. Although some members felt that issues associated with the school are secondary to the more global issues relating to the Graduate Council, concern was expressed regarding the impact of the proposed use of science labs and campus facilities as outlined in the proposal. The Council determined that it would have an interest in reviewing this matter, and the allocation of teaching assistants if the proposal moves forward.

Our response, coming the following month, was just slightly longer. Wanting not to be overly ambitious in the start-up years, we had arranged to open the charter school in facilities on the Thurgood Marshall College campus, which I controlled as provost. Further, we reiterated the agreement we had struck with the faculty who ran the wet labs in both the biology and chemistry departments, allowing charter school students to use UCSD laboratory facilities after hours and on weekends. Clearly, the issue for this committee boiled down to whether or not poor students from San Diego would intrude on the turf of faculty scientists at this public university.

On the other hand, the senate's Affirmative Action Committee was a unique committee of the faculty in that it included several staff members who ran various student diversity and recruitment programs on campus. Collectively, they feared that the mounting attention being devoted to the possibility of a charter school on campus targeting low-income students was simultaneously drawing negative attention to, and funds away from, their diversity programs—programs that had been unsuccessfully promising for more than a quarter of a century to make a difference in enrolling more African American and Latino students at the University of California.

The Affirmative Action Committee's report said, "[I]t is likely that the school will inevitably demand some human resources, in terms of UC faculty and staff involvement. Some of us feel that the demands on our time are already near overwhelming and suspect that this additional burden might result in our paying less attention to the well-being and academic success of UC students from diverse backgrounds…."

Our proposal assiduously avoided placing any demands on these UCSD personnel in the start-up and running of the school. The operating budget would allow us to hire the best teachers and administrative staff from surrounding school districts and the nation. Several UCSD faculty and staff members had voluntarily come forward to offer special enrichment lectures and career advising in order to complement the intellectual life of the charter school. Notable in this regard were concerned faculty from the San Diego Supercomputer Center, engineering departments, and numerous social science and humanities professors. It had been heartening to hear well-intentioned professors offering their time at the future school, even as their own faculty representatives had fought its establishment over the previous months. Nevertheless, our proposal called for a minimum of campus resources and for no diversion of existing UCSD outreach personnel.

The Affirmative Action Committee's report went on to point out the proliferation of campus outreach programs. Believing that many of the current campus outreach programs were ineffective, however, we called upon the Affirmative Action Committee to mount a review of all such programs to determine their effectiveness and make recommendations to the chancellor regarding revision or elimination of ineffective programs. Our suspicion was that our charter school would compete well when judged against the plethora of small-scale charismatic outreach programs that had existed on campus for the past thirty years. Despite several inquiries from the steering committee, there was to be no face-to-face meeting between the Affirmative Action Committee and any member of the steering committee. SP-1 had made their committee illegal, and I thought their abysmal record of recruiting and retaining minority students made them irrelevant as well.

Although I opposed doing away with affirmative action as a consideration in admissions, SP-1 did clear the air of some institutional hypocrisy. The proprietors of the affirmative action industry at the University of California were usually middle-aged ethnic minorities who seemed to begin most sentences of complaint with, "The white man this..." or "The white man that...." Almost on cue, most white men (and now, women) at the university hung their heads in responsive shame to commence an awkward defense of the institution's racism. This uniquely 1960's display of outrage and pitifulness had empowered the captains of the university's affirmative action industry to capture an intangible moral high ground, but few real victories for minority students. The ritual reduced legitimate white liberal power brokers to stammering apologies, even as it perversely kept real social solutions at bay. Former sixties radicals now had comfortable jobs in the university's affirmative action industry, and they were obviously reluctant to threaten their positions by actually acting affirmatively.

Similarly, several members of the Committee on Educational Policy (CEP) often used a peculiar brand of left wing verbiage in advocating the rights of the working classes and the poor. It was a rare moment, however, to witness a translation of those beliefs into concrete institutional policy. Our steering committee waged a failed battle to win their support. Their annual report dated October 28, 1997, featured one bulleted item that contained no verb but still managed to express the hypocrisy of the committee's position: "Proposal for a UCSD Charter High School (conditional support providing no outreach, instructional, or research funds used)."

The Planning and Budget Committee's report nibbled around the edges of the issue and, perhaps, best captured the ambiguity of the moment: "The best path for the campus, however, remains unclear to us."

Although the CEP report appeared more analytical and thorough, it was actually an exercise in obfuscation that posed a series of ridiculing interrogatives. The Planning and Budget Committee's report, on the other hand, was more raw, less sophisticated. It fretted about "untoward events" taking place between university students and the charter school adolescents. It worried that there would be competition between UCSD undergraduates and charter school students for resources and lab space. Such open declarations of institutional unwillingness to share public resources in a smart, productive way played right into our hands. I wondered aloud where the State of California would be if past UC faculty had declined to use any university resources to help California's agriculture.

If the Planning and Budget Committee report was unsophisticated, the written report of the Committee on Preparatory Education (CPE) was truly vulgar. Although struggling to be polite, CPE's reply conveyed the tone of a spanking. CPE's comments about the "weak emotional stamina of poor children," implying a fragile psychological makeup and an inability to attend school away from their families, were borne out of a latent paternalism. The report openly suggested that poor minority children needed academic support, but that the university with its powerful intellectual spirit was not the place to help these kids. In fact, the report suggested that the university would somehow trigger their mental collapse.

Perhaps the senate committee most directly relevant to our proposal was the Admissions Committee. When our proposal arrived, inattentive professors inhabited the committee. The urgency of the SP-1 environment pointedly demonstrated their incompetence for this complex moment. It was the Admissions Committee's responsibility to determine a framework for deciding which fortunate few of tens of thousands of families would be sent UC acceptance letters. The Admissions Committee's strategy seemed to be to weigh down our effort with an unrelenting diet of abstract rhetorical questions proffered to seem erudite, thoughtful, and preferably unanswerable. Their reply to our proposal communicated a sense of miserable dread and was peppered with concerns about maintaining the funding and emotional support for the campus' Early Academic Outreach Program (EAOP), part of the ineffective affirmative action industry. However, the report carefully avoided mentioning the possibility of authorizing a comparative evaluation of the university's ongoing recruitment and preparation efforts. The report instead stated that such a comparison would be, "unfair and inappropriate." The sentiment exemplified the unholy alliance of institutional conservatism protecting the ineffectual progressivism against which we struggled.

None of the nine reports constituted a fatal blow, but in combination they were a withering set of nibbling attacks aimed at discouraging us from bringing the project to fruition. Collectively, they hinted that if the proposal were voluntarily withdrawn, the campus would have more time and attention to address the core admissions issues raised by the charter school initiative.

A week after receiving them, I called an old friend in the UC General Counsel's Office in Oakland to unload my worries and fears. He felt that the effort was tragically over and that demanding a showdown with the UCSD Academic Senate was unwise. Although disagreeing on the virtue of proceeding, he and I simultaneously appreciated the toll of exhaustion the experience had exacted of all the participants. He cautioned that pushing further was no longer a strategy, but a sacrifice. The next day, I faxed him copies of the subcommittee reports blanketed by a melancholy cover letter of my own.

The protracted encounter with the committees of the UCSD Academic Senate was, nevertheless, successful in drawing out the official comments of the opponents. Andrew had, over the previous weeks, developed a working relationship with Jeff Ristine, the higher education reporter for San Diego's major newspaper, the

San Diego Union-Tribune. Despite my anger, I still felt conflicted about the idea of publicizing the hubris and passive racism of people who had been my colleagues, and in some cases friends, for over 25 years. Andrew felt no such conflict. He was an idealistic college student, bitterly disillusioned with a faculty he had idealized, mentors who were collectively failing to do the right thing. Within hours, copies of the embarrassing reports were in Ristine's hands.

We worked around the clock to fashion our replies to the damning reports. We crafted a response to speak to the members of the various senate committees, to the guardians of the affirmative action industry, and to those busy faculty who, at one time or another, thought that this whole mess—affirmative action, financial aid, admissions—was a distraction from their true mission of academic research. Our idea of the urban Educational Field Station, carrying on the tradition of Gilman and Kerr, was being treated as a distraction, perhaps a dangerous one, by most of the leadership at UCSD.

We had offered the proposal for comment and approval but had been rebuffed without a decision. The chair of the senate had packaged the various committee reports and assumed that, bled by a thousand small cuts, our proposal would be withdrawn and die a painful, preferably quiet death. And perhaps most important, no single committee or faculty member might be perceived to have delivered the mortal blow.

The cover letter containing the reports made no clear recommendation to the chancellor. Instead, the nine reports were left to stand as a malevolent barrier intended to halt our advance.

Within a week, however, we answered the negative reports point by point and simultaneously began preparations for a revised proposal, incorporating the more critical comments. The revised proposal was sent, once again, to the academic senate a month later, in late March. We had not gone away or faded in the face of opposition. We demanded an answer. That answer came swiftly and firmly. On April 23, 1997, the chair of the academic senate wrote:

In UCSD's case, it may make more sense to focus campus efforts on programs that have the widest scope and would directly affect the composition of the UC student body, rather than on a single secondary school of quite limited size. A minority of members of the Senate Council are of the opinion that a Charter High School of the kind proposed could be pursued, but only; 1) if it is a partnership between UCSD, the Governor, the Regents, the Office of the President, the San Diego Unified School District, and private donors, all of whom would share financial responsibility for sustaining it; 2) if financing of UCSD's share of the effort is not to be undertaken at the expense of other outreach initiatives that promise a broader solution to the problem of increasing the eligibility and competitiveness of students from disadvantaged populations in UC admissions. … The majority of the Senate Council for the reasons stated above, cannot at this point endorse the Charter High School proposal and does not recommend its approval by the Representative Assembly.

As we approached the formal vote of the UCSD Representative Assembly in May, the odds were clearly against us.

Chapter Four

Enter the White House

At about the same time the steering committee was resubmitting the proposal, I received a telephone call from UCSD political science professor, Sam Popkin, informing me that White House staffers were looking seriously at the UCSD commencement event as an occasion for President Bill Clinton to give his keynote *Race in America* speech. Sam had taken sabbatical leave to serve as a pollster for the Democratic party during the 1992 and 1996 presidential campaigns and was closely wired into the Clinton White House. Well known around the campus for his bravura and pluck, Sam was a steady, reliable source on White House thinking. Jesse Jackson and other Democratic leaders had been making it clear that President Clinton had to speak out against California's assault on the one social program most important to African Americans, affirmative action—and California had to be the venue.

According to Sam, Clinton's commencement speech at UCSD would kick off a year-long White House initiative outlining a three-pronged attack on racial inequality. First, the president would announce the formation of a seven-member Presidential Advisory Board on Race, which would then travel the country for a year gathering data and organizing town hall meetings to discuss race regionally. Next, during that same year, the president would commit one event per month to the topic of race. Finally, he would propose a new set of initiatives designed to enforce existing civil rights law and enact new legislation to deal with high unemployment, housing discrimination, and especially unequal access to education among minorities.

The debate over our charter school spotlighted Thurgood Marshall College and its progressive education and civic agenda in the statewide and national media, making UCSD an attractive location for a major speech about race at the time. The UCSD Charter High School proposal was the only constructive initiative to emerge from the University of California following the elimination of affirmative action. UCSD's proximity to the border, moreover, allowed the president to woo Latino voters by stressing the rights of immigrants.

Early in April, President Clinton's staff confirmed that he was coming to give UCSD's commencement address on June 14, and that he would deliver a blockbuster policy statement on race and affirmative action.

Because of articles appearing about the charter school debate in the *San Diego Union-Tribune* and the *Los Angeles Times*, it had become impossible for me to attend a cocktail party, go shopping, or sit in a restaurant without being asked to discuss the charter school proposal. The president's visit and his announced topic made what had been a regional story into a national event. Our charter school proposal was now wedged uncomfortably between Pete Wilson, Ward Connerly, SP-1, and Proposition 209 on one side, and presidential politics on the other. While hopeful, I was not sure that Clinton's visit was going to do our effort any favors; after all, he would be leaving town the next day.

Clinton's visit and the vote on the charter school sped towards an inevitable collision. The academic senate leadership's official recommendation not to endorse our school had lengthened the odds, but there was still a chance that the UCSD Representative Assembly would approve our moving forward. Bud, Pat, and the rest of the steering group were working hard to gather the votes we needed from among the 88 representative assembly members.

As the steering committee prepared a strategy for the May 6 faculty vote, the procedural move that scared us the most was the possibility that someone would call for a campus-wide mail ballot. We were confident that, left alone for two hours in an auditorium with a couple of hundred reasonably engaged colleagues, we could persuade them to see things our way. After all, none of our critics had been willing to make public statements opposing the project. All that we had were anonymous "committee reports." If the vote went beyond the senate's representative assembly to a plebiscite of all campus faculty, ignorance about the proposal would surely be a powerful force against us.

On April 24, 1997, less than a month before the May 6 showdown, Chancellor Dynes issued a statement to the members of the UCSD Representative Assembly. He politely complimented both the work of the UCSD Charter School Steering Committee and of our critics in the senate, excused himself from the upcoming meeting, and attempted to take the issue of resources off the table while remaining neutral toward the proposal itself. The new chancellor's carefully worded statement read, in part:

> I regret that due to a previous commitment in Oakland, I will not be able to join you on May 6th for the special meeting of the Academic Senate Representative Assembly. Because the UCSD Charter High School proposal is on the agenda for consideration, I want to encourage you to attend this meeting and participate in the discussion of this important item.
>
> During the review process, legitimate issues have been raised that warrant discussion. Among them is the question of the resources the UCSD campus would be required to commit to the Charter School if the proposal is approved. Given our many academic needs, we are unable to use any instruction and research funding for the charter school. Any support provided by the campus will be from expanded system-wide funding for K-12 outreach.
>
> The final decision on the creation of a UCSD charter school will depend on how the question of funding and other important issues raised during the review are resolved. I await your advice and recommendations with confidence that the process leading to the Representative Assembly's vote has been

thorough and rigorous.

This was, in fact, the second time that the chancellor had written to the senate to take the issue of UCSD funding for the charter school off the table. It went unheard, however. Faculty members continued to wage a whisper campaign about UCSD wasting its reputation and its money on a school for poor kids.

Oceanographer Freeman Gilbert once told me during a bumpy plane ride to Oakland something to the effect that "little people are afraid of big ideas." He had discovered the truth of this adage, he said, when some scientific colleagues narrowed their gaze not for precision, but rather out of intimidation before the broad ambiguities of life. Although he was speaking then about a very different subject and context, many years later, as May 6 approached, I recalled his words and the turbulence of the jet.

Because our charter students would remain in the public school system (unlike, for example, students in the school voucher programs), their Average Daily Attendance (ADA) funds would follow them and, under our proposal, pay for the operating expenses of the school. While this had been a provision of our proposal from the beginning, the chancellor's further assurance that UCSD funds would not be used for the school made our opponents' continued focus on that issue doubly disingenuous.

While tumbling toward the summer solstice, everyone seemed to feel that the campus, like the state and nation, was being pulled apart by its social convictions on one side and its shared academic responsibilities on the other. Our steering group desperately wanted to convey that our urban Educational Field Station would reconcile both, but battling the forces of rumor and confusion appeared almost hopeless. It was not clear whether the heightened buzz around Clinton's commencement address helped or hurt our cause.

Trepidation mounted as everyone contemplated what was at stake in this confrontation. The debate was no longer purely about the charter school. Despite its lofty title, a faculty senate is no more reliable a device for democracy than a mob. It is often led or influenced by the most persistent multi-syllabic bully.

In turning the charter school debate into an issue over joint governance between the faculty and administration, UCSD's Academic Senate got to have its cake and eat it too. By pressuring the new chancellor, faculty leaders might successfully intimidate him into killing the charter school proposal and help establish the precedent for a relationship in which they wielded more power with regard to future decisions. On the surface, joint governance was a noble instrument, furthering the highest principles of social democracy. Just beneath the surface, however, faculty leaders sought to provoke a malevolent response to a worthy, historically sound proposal under the benign auspices of participatory democracy.

Unlike the campus' chief executive, the senate works in relative obscurity and anonymity, sharing none of the political responsibility of having to explain to the public why the campus takes certain positions. It was a win-win strategy for the faculty opponents; the new chancellor was being backed into a corner, and the bullies were in no mood to show him either tolerance or mercy.

On the day before the meeting, the *San Diego Union-Tribune* ran a staff editorial entitled "UCSD's Obligation To Serve." It summed up what was at stake:

> Indeed, a dismaying air of elitism appears to be a major factor behind the opposition of many (UCSD) faculty members to the creation on campus of a charter high school for low-income students...
>
> To be fair, not everyone at UCSD embraces this narrow-minded view. Chancellor Robert Dynes has supported the charter school as a key component of his commendable effort to involve the university more deeply in the San Diego region. The proposal also has the strong backing of Cecil Lytle, Provost of UCSD's Thurgood Marshall College, and a host of influential current and former faculty members and major benefactors of the university.
>
> Still, a vote set for tomorrow by the Academic Senate's elected representatives could go either way.
>
> The charter school plan offers UCSD an uncommon opportunity to serve San Diego. The proposal deserves even

more vigorous support from Chancellor Dynes if he hopes to realize his goal of developing a close relationship between the university and the region. More to the point, if members of the Academic Senate reject this worthy project, they will fail their obligation to serve San Diego.

The Showdown

On the day of the representative assembly vote, Bud seemed especially anxious. On the other hand, I felt strangely calm and ready to commence the hand-to-hand combat. I realized that this May 6 meeting represented a do-or-die situation for our proposal and for me. If approved, we were free to begin the arduous work of raising money for the building and submitting the finished proposal to the San Diego Unified School District for their own laborious process of approval. And after that, of course, we would have to form a governance board, find an architect, appoint a principal, hire teachers, buy equipment, recruit students, and deal with busing, lunches, sports, dances, and all of the other myriad aspects of a real high school. The words of General Eisenhower on the morning of D-Day ran through my head: "If we are successful today, our troubles are only beginning."

The battle in the faculty senate over the mission of the university had diverted more time and energy away from the real tangible aspects of the school's planning than anyone could have anticipated. It was the topic of every faculty meeting and dinner party. "Where are you on the charter school?" had become the opening gambit of every conversation; it was a non-rhetorical inquiry into each professor's astrological standing in the campus' political cosmos. But now the time had come for the senate to vote its conscience.

I spent the night before experiencing great doubt and trepidation. However the meeting might turn out, this conflagration was going to leave deep indelible scars on the campus and on me. I knew that, either way, the campus already looked selfish and self-centered in its vitriolic criticism of the project. For the first time in this four-year effort, I began to wonder if we were right, and if it was worth risking the reputation of the university to prove a point. Reason and self-preservation told me that I couldn't afford the luxury of self-doubt as I prepared to address the representatives of the UCSD faculty in a roomful of aggressive ambivalence.

Unknown to me, Andrew had organized a noisy and impromptu demonstration outside the UCSD Academic Senate Office before the meeting. He excitedly rushed up to me as I paced the hallway outside Garren Auditorium. As the story of the demonstration unfolded in my ear, it was clear that his motivation up the stairs was inspired by two campus police officers outside who appeared to be in hot pursuit.

Apparently, the authorities had been ordered to prevent unauthorized members of the public from entering the meeting room, and an officer had informed Andrew that as a member of the general public, he was to be kept out. I launched into my familiar speech about how students couldn't use violence or provocations in their protests while he, using me for cover, brazenly passed the two sentries at the double door and entered the faculty senate meeting. He took a seat beside me.

The record overflow crowd for a faculty senate meeting was directed from Garren to Leibow Auditorium on the next level up, where they could watch the proceedings on closed circuit TV. Judging by the jostling and crowding in the hallway and on the stairs leading to Leibow, the turnout was going to be more than either of the big lecture halls could handle. Garren Auditorium was divided into three groups of fixed seats. The center rows were reserved for the voting members of the representative assembly, while the left- and right-hand rows held other attending, nonvoting faculty. Approved members of the general public, including the press, were seated in the back.

In one corner of the narrow hallway outside Garren, the press was arguing with senate staff about bringing cameras and cables into the room. In another, curious medical students wandering from class to class wondered what all of the fuss was about.

Once the meeting came to order, the assembly dispensed with prefatory items on the agenda. The overflow crowd and shouting protesters outside gave this mundane business an air of the absurd. Everyone knew that the real event was the showdown between the proponents and opponents of the charter school proposal. It was guaranteed to be great academic theater: either a lynching or a coronation.

The chair of the academic senate approached the microphone. After some preliminary introductions, he nervously set upon the matter that drew everyone there. He glared at me, then attempted a smile, and finally introduced the charter school proposal.

For the next several minutes, he freely recited from the negative reports of the faculty committees. Then he reminded everyone there that the faculty did, indeed, share governance of the campus with the new chancellor. I sat with as stony a face as I could muster until he concluded: "And so the decision lies with the representative assembly, a decision that will be the recommendation to Chancellor Dynes who, from the beginning, has made clear his intention to respect the rule of the senate as our longstanding tradition of shared governance requires. I would like to call now on Provost Lytle to speak on behalf of the proposal to establish a charter high school on the UCSD campus and to make a motion."

As he spoke, I reviewed my notes and rehearsed what I would say and how I would say it. It was the only way to confine my rage. Bud had cautioned me to mask my anger and frustration behind a veneer of insistent politeness. But I had lost my patience with the endless encounters and questions about the proposal—both questions in the parking lot and questions in the meeting rooms—that masked a deep, unacknowledged institutional racism. In a moment, I would be standing in front of five hundred or so mostly white people who would prefer that both I and the problem I brought them would simply disappear. But what exactly was the problem that I had brought them? What exactly did this little school symbolize to so many of my colleagues?

In a moment, the son of an African American janitor from New York City would be standing before the assembled faculty of the University of California, San Diego, most of whom had been in school nearly all of their lives. Few, if any, had tended bar, sold real estate, driven a cab, or punched a clock with any regularity. My task was to present two courses of action: continue to burnish naive feelings of valiant, but failed, 1960s liberalism, or trust the more pragmatic vision represented by our proposal. I had not come to beg for the establishment of a charter school, but to plead with the University of California, San Diego to display the courage of its convictions.

As I got up to walk to the podium I was startled by the loud applause and standing ovation that greeted me from the public gallery. I was more accustomed to the stony atmosphere of committee rooms where I struggled against the quiet strangulation of our idea.

The meetings of the UCSD Academic Senate are solemn occasions, usually measured in quality by the quantity of obscure and grandiose words bellowed from the back of the auditorium or the clever turns of phrase muttered quietly from the front rows. It was always a room full of very smart people. This afternoon, it was full of hundreds of very anxious, smart people.

My task was to present the conceptual overview of the proposal. Bud, the campus academic expert on schools, would follow with the details as well as the goals and objectives. I couldn't appear scolding, but as Bill McGill told me two nights earlier, "Look them straight in the eye and tell the truth." Walter Kudumu and his pointed index finger had implored me to, "Put it on 'em."

From behind the mask, I listened to my own voice give the six-minute speech I had rehearsed so many times on our long four-year journey to the floor of the UCSD Academic Senate.

At the end, squaring my shoulders, I then said the words that would start the final debate. "I have been reminded by Professor Alden Mosshammer, senate parliamentarian, that a motion must be placed before the representative assembly before discussion can take place," I said, looking at my colleagues around the room. "I move that the UCSD Representative Assembly approve and recommend to the chancellor the establishment of the UCSD Charter High School as proposed."

I took my seat next to Andrew while the gallery again applauded, and Bud rose to give his expert position on the research supporting our idea—to quell some final academic jitters, we hoped.

As the debate ensued, more and more faculty spoke, mostly in favor of the charter school. Some questioned specific aspects of the project, I suspected, more for the purpose of demonstrating that they had actually read the proposal. Few of our opponents even then believed enough in the strength of their criticism to rise publicly. One economist claimed to have had a prior engagement, but he had a colleague read a prepared statement about how the charter school failed a cost/benefit analysis since its graduates might attend colleges other than UCSD.

Professor after professor stood in front of the microphone testing one theoretical assumption after another about the world outside the gates of the university. It was blithely assumed that academic rank and privilege gave one special insight into the lives of the less fortunate who would be served by this school. Moreover, each speaker, pro and con, felt that their opinion was an important empirical observation that should be acted upon.

Bill McGill had been adamant that we should not scold the faculty. He apparently gave no such instruction to the students. John Lien, one of my provost's interns, was a sincere student who hated the hypocrisy being displayed by the faculty opponents. He had been a quiet warrior in the office—preparing documents, finding research, and keeping his eyes and ears open during meetings. A Vietnamese American who spoke passionately and directly, John eloquently supported the project even as his presence at the microphone demonstrated that our initiative had support beyond the African American and Mexican American communities.

Lyndsey Lovelace, a talented first-year Thurgood Marshall College student, was the last person from the public gallery authorized by the senate to speak, and she made the most compelling remarks. She grew up in a tough L.A. neighborhood but had the opportunity to attend a high school where the teachers believed in their students and prepared them for college. "I'm the reason you have to support this school," she said, "and others like me."

Both she and John made deep impressions because they were young, idealistic, and still saw the world in the enviably simple terms of right and wrong. Faculty are the natural "tormentors" of students, and the latter take delight in an any opportunity to expose the vulnerabilities of their "oppressors." For John and Lyndsey, I was right and the faculty opponents were wrong. These two innocents were not going to pass up a chance to publicly point out just how hypocritical the faculty opposition had been.

Things Fall Apart

Lyndsey finished and there was some hasty shuffling of papers as a din began to rise from the audience. "What do we do?" "Where's the ballot?" "Which ballot did you say?" "I want to speak!" "The discussion's over. Let's vote, damn it!" "What exactly are we voting for?"

The tension that had held everyone in their seats for the past two hours was quickly uncoiling into chaos, the meeting was rapidly spinning out of control. UCSD's Academic Senate now exposed its angry, vainglorious—and humorous—underbelly.

"Remember that the motion on the floor," the chair shouted into the microphone (causing high-pitched feedback), "is the request to the representative assembly to endorse the proposal that has been submitted by the steering committee to establish a charter high school on the campus." He could barely be heard over the din. "The vote should be 'yes,' 'no,' or 'abstain.' One of them! Not all three of them!" I thought he seemed rattled as individual faculty stood at their seats directing questions and curses at the front of the room and at each other. "I repeat," he cried, clutching the mike in both hands, "if you are not a member of the representative assembly, you should not vote. And if you are an alternate and the representative is here, you should not vote either!"

A mathematician rose to decry the negative influence high school students would have on the university's mission. The founding chair of pediatrics countered by loudly pronouncing, "Adolescence is not a contagious disease." An eminent psychiatrist launched into a bitter denunciation of the *San Diego Union-Tribune's* conservative slant and its surprising support for the project to aid disadvantaged youngsters. Andrew's eyes widened a bit as he silently took it all in.

"Which ballot do we use?" "I don't have a ballot!" The male-dominated cacophony continued until a shrill voice suddenly screeched over the PA system: "While the vote is being tabulated... Listen! While the vote...Hey, wait a minute. Listen! While the vote is being tabulated and before the outcome is known, I'd like to make a motion, and let me read it to you." The chair of the Committee for Educational Policy had stepped in front of the befuddled chair of the academic senate to make a pre-arranged motion. Because of the timbre and volume of her voice, she quieted the crowd sufficiently to proceed.

Just as she began, however, a professor from the middle of the room raised an index finger and shouted, "Mr. Chairman! Point of Order! You can't have two motions on the floor at the same time. Point of Order, Mr. Chairman! Georgios, Point of Order, Please!"

The CEP chair paused to look up from the paper she held close to her face. I noticed a slight tremor in her hand that was rattling the half-page, hastily torn from a yellow legal pad. Although much of what she said was nearly inaudible, it was clear that this pre-planned public statement was about the good intentions of UCSD's faculty towards disadvantaged and minority youth. It must have been intended to provide cover when the charter school proposal was voted down. The event only added to the confusion.

She launched into a second reading of the ill-timed motion, oblivious to the contagious chaos continuing to spread around the room. She read, increasing in volume and speed, until the statement was all but unintelligible. When finished, she crumbled the paper that contained her motion and abruptly sat down, leaving the senate chair standing alone, again gazing out, bewildered, at a threatening rabble that used to be the UCSD faculty. He stepped over to the parliamentarian to confer about the strange situation of having two motions open simultaneously.

The senate leaders' curious no-huddle strategy was backfiring. Apparently, the charter school proposal would not die quietly. As the chair returned to the microphone; the din diminished to isolated grumbling. He was trying to speak to the assemblage and, at the same time, continue a bifurcated conversation with the parliamentarian to the right of the microphone, checking on each statement he was making over the PA system.

By now, however, the 300 or so people who were upstairs viewing the proceedings on closed circuit TV were congregating downstairs in the hallways and aisles. Theirs had been a one-way conversation so far; they now wanted their voices heard, too. What had been merely an exercise in confusion was becoming a dangerous situation as people pressed against the walls, stumbling over each other and the steps leading down the aisles.

"I'm informed by the parliamentarian," the senate chair said, "that we cannot vote on this motion." "Which motion?" someone interrupted. "The second motion. I'm sorry," he continued without looking up, "—until the results are out. But I'm told that we can have a discussion on the second motion while we're waiting to tabulate Provost Lytle's motion."

I rose from my seat to say that this was very confusing. "Why don't we wait a few minutes until the paper ballots are collected?" The chair cut me off by turning to the parliamentarian and asking over the microphone, "Is there anything else?"

At that moment, a largely unknown chemistry professor strode toward the front of the auditorium, violently grabbed the microphone, and presented her point of view: "I am a European! When I arrived in this country, I was appalled by the poor quality, the state of education in this country. How do kids learn anything here? Yes, I am an elitist and I think this proposal is wrong. We are here to educate the best and the brightest, and this idea will fail. Why are we talking about this?"

The professor had expressed what many in the room felt but were afraid to articulate. This was not the traditional liberal lament, it was an embarrassing expression of the gulf that existed between the self-serving satisfaction the faculty enjoyed in the comfort of a great public research university and the need to act on personal conviction. During the breathless moment following her brief stuttering outburst, there was prodigious squirming. The faculty was uncomfortable with such a raw display of their own unspoken trepidation.

Peter Irons had been waiting just behind her to speak at the microphone and broke the awkward silence with a sarcastic reference to honoring elitism. Then Professor Irons, an outstanding lawyer and author of *May It Please the Court* and other distinguished works of political science, spoke about the need for the university to be creative and bold in addressing the appalling undereducation of low-income high school students.

Although clearly violating parliamentary order, these last voices had given our motion a final buffet of support even as the voting assembly members were filling out their ballots.

The senate secretary collected and tallied the folded bits of paper during the quietest minutes of the evening. Then she handed a sheet of paper to the chair. This was it—he had the final vote and our fate in his hands.

He looked down and fingered the paper while we all held our breath. He made several halting gestures toward a chalkboard with the words "FOR," "AGAINST," and "ABSTENTIONS" on it, but failed to write anything. Suddenly, he turned back to the assembly and said, "The Lytle Motion passes 36 For, 23 Against, and 3 Abstentions."

Cheering and applause erupted from the gallery forward. Turning to write down the numbers, the chair scrawled, "23 FOR, 36 AGAINST, and 3 ABSTENTIONS." Jubilation changed to earnest shouts pointing out his error. He seemed more disoriented than ever until the secretary whispered his interpolation of the figures into his ear. He rubbed out the errors with the sleeve of his well-worn blazer, and then rewrote the numbers in the correct order. Jeers turned back to jubilation again as some people started to leave the room. Our charter school had passed.

Bud raised his hand and made the motion to adjourn. Someone seconded.

Just then, at the height of our victory, the elitism-honoring chemistry professor returned to the microphone and called for a campus-wide mail ballot. Our opponents' final gambit had emerged. Bud furrowed his brows and rose to address the parliamentarian and the chair, "A motion to adjourn has been made—it supersedes other motions. Do we even have quorum anymore?" No one in the front of the room paid any attention to him as they called for a vote on holding a mail ballot. The motion passed.

Bill excused himself as the other members of the steering committee headed to the campus pub. "What have we done? We might have to actually build this thing!" laughed Bud as he poured us each a glass. Pat grinned and toasted our success.

Although I celebrated with them, dread nagged at me. I could not help but feel that although we had just won, we might still be doomed.

The Mail Ballot

As promised, the mail ballot arrived on the desks of UCSD's 1,345 faculty members a week later. The ballot was a simple one-page history of the May 6 representative assembly vote. It also included instructions for how to fill out the ballot "For" or "Against." There was the usual written admonition at the bottom of the page to sign it and return it to the Academic Senate Office, "…no later than 4:30 P.M., on Wednesday, June 4, 1997." Attached were two combative position statements, one pro and one con.

Every member of the steering committee campaigned hard. Sensing the need for a positive ratchet, UCSD alumnus (and Pat's former student) Peter Preuss pledged $500,000 towards the building fund, hoping to allay faculty fears about the prospects of raising the money for the building. The *San Diego Union-Tribune* and the *Los Angeles Times* ran several articles and editorials supporting the UCSD Charter High School effort and announcing the cash pledge. One of the network news affiliates in San Diego aired an editorial, as well. But it all rested on the will of an independent faculty with a well-honed irreverence for public opinion.

The steering committee met two days before the mail ballot dead-line. We gathered like a platoon of shell-shocked troops made weary by sustained combat. We didn't know whether we had won or lost.

Andrew arrived a few minutes late, badly sunburned and carrying a clipboard. He sat on the stuffed chair and met Bill McGill's supercilious gaze. "What have you got there?" asked Bill.

"I organized a petition drive—I think I have over a thousand signatures here from UCSD students in support of the school. Maybe we can use it with the chancellor if the ballot is close…"

"Names are cheap, kid," Bill declared. Andrew slyly dropped the clipboard under his chair and kicked it out of sight.

While still striving for victory, I would have simply and quietly welcomed any form of retreat from the stress of the past four years. We were all exhausted, and we could not escape the feeling that within the next twenty-four hours we would either be rescued or forced to surrender. There were many occasions when I could have pulled the plug on the project and have been credited for "bringing up a good idea." But I had pushed and pushed against considerable odds for a principle from which retreat proved to be impossible.

Although we were a steering committee, I had brought the idea forward, it was my energy that sustained the effort, and I was out on a limb that I felt I had created all by myself. I had personalized the struggle. For me, it was about being a black man in a highly insular, white male dominated culture that murdered both ideas and people it found threatening to its existence. For me, it was no longer only about championing opportunities for the kids. I regarded the project as an epic struggle between good and evil, informed daring and blind neglect, black and white.

Ultimately, it was about my pride.

But now there were few scenarios left to play out, and even fewer options. It was late afternoon, so I uncorked a bottle of red wine that had languished from a faculty reception the week before. Everyone silently accepted a glass except Bill, who worried aloud about aggravating his mild case of diabetes. It was the first time I had heard of his ailment or ever associated Bill McGill with any form of weakness or vulnerability.

I had withheld one personal revelation from the group. But now the warmth of the wine combined with my near teary-eyed exhaustion loosened my tongue enough to utter a final *res judicata*. As they sipped in silence, I told them that, in the event of a negative vote, I saw no way out for me other than to resign as provost of Thurgood Marshall College.

I was too tired to protest any more and felt that if the faculty were so callous as to turn back this effort without having any discussion or ideas for an alternative, I would be too discredited to remain among them as one of their titular leaders. I also knew that if this initiative went down, I would be one of the two or three UCSD leaders expected to go into the community to explain the campus decision. Frankly, I couldn't satisfactorily explain to myself the opposition, and I knew that it would be impossible for me to find the words to exonerate the UCSD faculty.

Walter Kudumu was his usually frank self and asked, "What you gonna do?" I replied that I was not sure, but that I felt that I had been as useful to the campus as I could be. I was out of ideas and energy.

Bud, I mused, must have quietly welcomed the thought that I might resign. It would alleviate the pressure I had continually put on him to stay out in front with me on the project. He would want the relief, I thought. Rafael was more disappointed and felt threatened, I believe. He and I had worked very closely together at Thurgood Marshall College and weathered a number of storms and controversies establishing the college's new core curriculum (Diversity, Justice, and Imagination), public service courses, a summer bridge program for minority students, and the name change for the college.

Bill, however, was more silent and pained. In my own selfish reverie, I did not anticipate or notice his anguish. He had lived through upheavals like this before. My willingness to fall on my sword brought back memories of earlier campus miseries. He had endured fights and losses at UCSD over Herbert Marcuse and the opening of Third College, and the fatal clashes at Columbia over the Vietnam War. He had returned to bucolic La Jolla, settling into his sunset years to witness yet another carnage about to take place. He had guided me through my administrative adventures with the college that he had helped to birth three decades earlier. The stinging sound of campus cannon fire was familiar to him and brought back his own unbearable sorrow.

I stayed in the office long after they left to clean up my desk and prepare for what the next few days might bring.

On June 5, I canceled my appointments in order to stay home and anxiously await the telephone call. When I was not throwing up, I was sobbing uncontrollably. It did not take a prodigious imagination to predict a negative outcome for the mail ballot. It was much too easy for faculty members to simply scribble "No," seal the envelope, and mail in the rejection without facing the responsibility of stating their purpose or defending their action. At 6:15 P.M. that evening the senate chair called. Although my head and heart held out hope, my gut already signaled the true outcome—the faculty who chose to vote had rejected our proposal, 293 in favor to 328 against. A mere 35 votes divided victory from defeat.

The first call I made that evening was to Bud. We played out all of the "what if's," then hung up the telephone, sighing that it was now all up to the chancellor. It was a fact that he currently had before him two advisory votes: the favorable, and better informed, May 6 vote of the representative assembly and; now, the narrowly contested June 4 mail ballot. My public role was over. There were to be no more votes to cultivate, no more committees to woo, and certainly no more revisions of the proposal to prepare. I had to rely on Bob Dynes' conscience.

The matter truly rested on the shoulders of the chancellor. Unlike the senate, however, Dynes was under enormous pressure from the press, politicians, and the public to overrule the most recent faculty mail ballot. He had few options and even less time to consider them. The senate called for a special meeting on Tuesday, June 10, to learn the chancellor's official reaction: Would he honor the notion of "shared governance" and bow to the will of the courtesan faculty, or would he follow the advice of the *San Diego*

Union-Tribune's June 9 editorial titled "Buck the Backlash?":

> In many ways, the charter school proposal is a test of the character of UCSD. Will the university remain a largely insular community of privileged academicians, or will it step up to its obligation to serve the larger San Diego region? With so much at stake, Chancellor Dynes cannot afford to retreat to the sidelines.

If he had any doubt of the importance placed on this project by state officials, statements in the national press by Ward Connerly and Pete Wilson removed it. They made the case in the print media and on television all that week that money would not be an obstacle, and that they were prepared to bankroll the building and operating costs.

Both the academic senate chair and Dynes asked me to withdraw the proposal from consideration before the chancellor's statement scheduled for June 10. I refused and continued to implore Dynes to reject the faculty's advisory vote and "buck the backlash." I began to wonder, 'If I'm so defeated, why are they asking for my gentle acquiescence?' They wanted the issue to simply fade away. Moreover, they wanted me to make it easy for them by taking the matter off the table. I refused every plea to retreat and waited, like everyone else, to see what the chancellor would do.

The academic senate meeting on Tuesday, June 10, took place late in the afternoon. The setting sun shone through the stained glass windows of Robinson Auditorium, painting faint shadowy images of what I fancied were gallows crawling up the far eastern wall. Although several hundred faculty members, students, and members of the press attended the meeting, no one chose to sit beside me. Even Bud was two rows ahead in the front. Bill customarily sat in the rear to observe a drama he had seen many times before.

My sense of isolation was now palpable and frightening. I had put myself at risk and taken the reputation of my college with me. It would not be just my loss, but also a defeat of the ideals and aspirations of Third College and the tradition of the Lumumba-

Zapata Demands that I had sought to translate into a palatable, less hysterical terminology. The circle had been inexorably narrowing and it was now over—like a fallen Roman patrician before the emperor, my only choice was in manner of death.

In the bizarre moment after the chancellor appeared but before he spoke, I thought about running out of the room. I thought about how I had spent the first half of the last decade watching helplessly as my beautiful wife of thirty years slowly died from cancer. This school was her idea. I thought about how I wasted the second half of the decade in this seemingly endless entanglement. I sat alone and I thought of the enormity of the waste.

"I'd like to call the meeting to order with the approval of the minutes of the last meeting," said the senate chair. After calling on the chancellor for remarks, he returned to his seat, I thought, barely hiding his contempt. Many of our longtime foes nodded their approval at the chancellor's first words: "The UCSD Charter High School proposal is dead!"

Chapter Five

Ashes, Ashes

I could not bring myself to call Bill later that evening. I was certain those words still rang in his ears. Although he had seen it all before, I sensed that this defeat conveyed agonizing memories. The liberating utopia he had tried to create out of a deep belief in the democratic values of public education—the same liberating utopia that was his salvation as the son of immigrants—came crashing down once again. This time, it was not the errant habits of young idealistic socialists who brought about defeat. Rather, this defeat was perpetrated by the malignant ignorance of frightened men and women whose chief occupational mission should have been to follow the motto of the University of California, "Let there be light." I knew that the pain of this sage was deep, intense, and final.

All Fall Down

Not only had I sought his advice, I had teased him with the offer of one last chance to lower the walls of a bastion he had grown up in, was nurtured by, and had helped to build. The charter school was the institutional solution he had groped for during the challenges of the Lumumba-Zapata Demands. He joined me in this campaign because of the curative appeal of the initiative and because maybe, just maybe, he thought that we could pull off now what he and many others had failed to achieve a generation earlier.

The taste of ashes was more bitter knowing that this kind old warrior may have been mortally wounded by one defeat too many. I no longer had the stamina to console the friend and teacher who was enticed to believe in one more effort to humanize and realize the redemptive ambitions he expected of his public university. It was a call that I should have made, and my failure to reach out to him at that moment was a supreme act of self-indulgence and cowardice.

By the end of the last call I did make that night, I knew I was alone. I had withheld my own personal loss and grief by throwing myself into establishing this school as some kind of private memorial. For five years, I had been afraid to blink, take a breath, stand at ease, or feel the wind. The present circumstance demanded that I suddenly now grieve over Rebecca's death and this failed resurrection. For the first time in my life, I was alone and without momentum. The grotesque howl that had been suppressed within me for so long, slowly took form. It was familiar and uninvited, but not to be denied any longer.

Unconsciously, I had been composing my letter of resignation for several days. By the time I actually sat at the computer that night, it was already in its second or third iteration—purged of much of the anger and angst that gave it birth.

My son Eric pleaded with me over the telephone earlier that evening not to quit. He said that I had already made my point and that the university would respond favorably, someday. I was not as confident.

The letter found its way to the chancellor's desk early the next morning. I briefly met with my staff at 10:00 A.M., but broke down before I could properly finish my apology and my farewell. Their applause rang in my ears as I rushed past some reporters who were waiting in the hallway. I took refuge in a downtown café, but was driven out by the curious stares from behind folded newspapers before my eggs arrived. My picture stared out at me from the front page of the *San Diego Union-Tribune*, over my condemnation, in quotes, of the university leadership—"Gutless and unimaginative."

I went to the one place where I felt the safest.

The high promontory of the back lawn of San Diego Hospice offered gusts of warm June wind and a panorama from the ocean on the west to the mountains on the east. The few people I passed were enduring their newly owned grief. They understood and knew the countenance of loneliness and death. I gave up my unread newspaper to an ancient man who joined me on the bench overlooking Mission Valley. We greeted each other without making eye contact, a simple nod sufficed for small talk. His presence made no impression on me until I felt his eyes turn towards me, searching my face. I had been too deep in my own thoughts to notice that he was clad only in a bathrobe and slippers, and that he clung awkwardly to a wheeled tripod dripping into him what I guessed to be pain killer. I realized that this man was soon to die.

His shy gaze made me nervous and temporarily jarred me out of my isolation. He moved closer, wrenching the high contraption over the uneven ground. I squirmed, wanting to be alone as he started humming. He moved beyond prudence and into my personal space. Why was he staring at me? I was not fearful or even curious; I just wanted to be left alone. But he was not humming. He was grunting—staring directly across my profile and trying to speak. Tugging my jacket, he formed semi-coherent phrases with a mixture of grunts and gestures.

I cursed my earlier nod as too provocative. "What is it? I have to leave, you can keep the paper," I muttered. With some irritation, I averted my eyes even further across the expanse below.

He crossed my gaze with the newspaper, pointing at my salty beard protruding from the front page—but still I looked away. The grunts continued and he demanded recognition and a reply. Finally turning to him in exasperation, my eyes fell not on his face but on the abundance of bandages encircling his throat.

As I gleaned from the next twenty minutes of gestures and proto-sounds, he was in the last throes of various metastasized cancers, concluding most recently and vainly with surgery to remove malignant lumps found in his throat. Despite all of this, he was interested in me and in my story. Over the next hour, he filled the air with grunts and gestures that conveyed to me that he was a retired schoolteacher and had followed the UCSD Charter High

School saga for the past four years. He, too, wanted to know what was going to happen.

I helped him adjust his robe when the sun moved directly above us, and his gesturing became even more animated and articulate. His croaking voice managed to indicate that he had wanted to meet me to express his support. His hands somehow told me that he wanted me to stay on and continue the fight. I told him that I could not continue. He wanted to know why I was there at the hospice, and I explained that my wife had died there. He wrote on a pad that he carried in his waist pocket, "You miss her?" It was both a question and a statement. To both, I nodded in desolate agreement. We stopped talking and sat silently gazing at the sea or into our hands.

When I returned home, there were several messages from Bill McGill. Each had a pleading tone imploring me to change my mind about resigning. Each word was separated by anguished heavy pauses asking me to call him. He called a meeting of the Charter School Steering Committee for the next day at which he delivered his plea in person. We adjourned with his promise to call everyone after he met with Bob Dynes later in the morning. His shuttle diplomacy did little to change my mind and I apologized for failing him.

Later, the *San Diego Union-Tribune* asked me for an opinion piece to explain my views on this defeat. The effort was over and, although exhausted by rage, I did not want to see the university trashed anymore in the papers. Despite the recent petty and short-sighted behavior of the faculty on this issue, I was a creature of the campus and did not want it savaged. UCSD still ran the county hospital caring for the uninsured, our alumni continued to transform biotech industries around the state, thousands of our students each year went on to top graduate programs throughout the country, and faculty research continued to enlighten all aspects of civic life. I did, however, want to set the record straight about the nature and quality of the debate that had taken place.

"The 18-month campus and public debate about the charter school," I wrote, "has not been a noble moment in our campus' brief history. It had been my hope—and remains so now—that campus leaders might raise not only the stakes but elevate our gaze beyond the typical ramparts higher education instinctively erects between the world of privilege and the broader community."

Despite attempts to soften the tone, UCSD took a beating in the press in the days between the chancellor's pronouncement that the charter school was DOA and President Clinton's visit. Political cartoons lampooned the faculty as false, selfish hypocrites more interested in maintaining an aloof, elitist status than in helping their community. The chancellor came in for particular ridicule as weak and indecisive. One drawing featured him raising a broken sword, dressed as Napoleon, seated backwards on a horse labeled "UCSD," and yelling "Forward!"

Hail to the Chiefs

It was now June 11, and Clinton would arrive on the 14th. His UCSD commencement speech had been planned for months, and he would name the members of a new Presidential Advisory Board on Race the following day, June 12, in preparation for the address. But his perfect venue was now a disaster area.

Ann Lewis, director of communications at the White House, called me to sort out what was happening. She had already phoned late in May wanting to know if the local turmoil would "step on the president's message." I told her then what she already knew—that it was too late to pull out, and that the president's avid support for the charter school movement was widely known and applauded. I suggested that the president could present his scripted message without any reference to the San Diego tragedy.

"If he's asked by the press, what do you think he should say?" she said.

"Ann, I'm the last one who should give Bill Clinton advice on what to say. Perhaps, he should say that he continues to support the establishment of charter schools as an effective tool to improve the education of children too often left behind. That's consistent with his record and skirts taking sides in our skirmish. What do you think?"

"I'll get back to you" she said and hung up. Ann was a veteran of the Democratic ethnic politics of Boston and knew her way in and out of controversy. Her inquiry, I found out much later, was really an attempt to gauge my temperament and whether or not I might make things more uncomfortable for the president during his highly publicized visit. An hour later, a fax rolled out of the office machine with a one-line insertion referencing charter schools that was to be planted in his speech. I faxed back a slight revision that was closer to the facts in our case. Twenty minutes later Ann called back with a third revision. The difference, I thought, was negligible, but she was scrupulously planning every word, as she knew they would be intensely scrutinized by the media for any signal of his policy or personal intentions. I said fine, and that was that.

I had made myself a pariah among the campus administration and faculty. The intense contact I had had with the members of the committees for the past two years suddenly broke off. But at least I was not the chancellor.

His last words on the matter, "The UCSD Charter High School proposal is dead," had become a noose for him. Although seeking to appease a dozen or more truculent faculty senate members, the severity of his words echoed far beyond UCSD.

Published in the *San Diego Union-Tribune* June 16, 1997   © Dave Kellett

On commencement day, I sat on stage with twenty other dignitaries facing an audience of 22,000 cheering people not knowing just how I felt. About 4,000 were there to graduate, another 10,000 or so were there to beam with pride over the success of their graduates, and the rest were there to see the president of the United States. I had resigned just days earlier, yet, out of respect for my students, I attended this very public occasion in deep personal despair.

About half the graduating seniors and an equal number of faculty members wore colorful "Save The Charter School" buttons on their black gowns. The defeat of the charter school proposal had cast a shadow over the president's intention to defend affirmative action even before he had spoken, and a sense of tension was palpable amidst the joy of graduation day.

Lieutenant Governor Gray Davis, Regent Ward Connerly, and President Clinton sat on the dais with the chancellor, UC President Richard Atkinson, Bill McGill, and a few other faculty leaders, including myself and the faculty senate chair, all dressed in our full academic regalia. Clinton, to signal the seriousness of his intent, had seated on the dais and in the surrounding audience two United States senators, Barbara Boxer and Dan Akaka; seven congressmen, including civil rights hero John Lewis; five of his cabinet secretaries, including Secretary of Education Richard Riley; UN Ambassador Bill Richardson; and a host of other dignitaries. including Thurgood Marshall, Jr. The absurdity of it struck me. My faculty adversaries, like me, were little more than scenery, an emblazoned backdrop against which others would hold their passion play.

The senate chair gave one of several introductory speeches and attempted to dismiss some of the tension by joking about the inability of tenured professors to agree on anything.

Although it seemed a few days too late, Clinton had raised the stakes of the occasion by choosing our campus for a major policy speech on race. Without a doubt, he was showing that he intended something to happen with regard to the questions surrounding affirmative action. His timing was impeccable. The University of California the previous year was the scene of the first national refutation of affirmative action policy with the infamous UC regents SP-1 order and the subsequent passage of California's Proposition 209 by state ballot. Here, he could lecture Pete Wilson (who boycotted the ceremony) and Ward Connerly on their misguided tactics.

Connerly glowered at the president. He chose to attend because he knew he would be on national television following the president's speech to counter Clinton's "mend it, don't end it" notions about affirmative action.

Despite the heraldry of commencement and the excitement surrounding an address by the president of the United States, it was the ten-minute speech by Coleen Sabatini, student body president and Thurgood Marshall College senior, given before Clinton's address, that roused the crowd. She was forceful, articulate, and very bright. Her powerful endorsement for an on-campus charter school for poor children brought the assembled students, and a larger number of the faculty than I would have supposed, to their feet.

Clinton, the consummate rhetorician, opened his speech by referring to her passionate words and to the senate chair's cool dismissal of our local controversy. "Well, ladies and gentlemen, the first thing I would like to say is that Coleen spoke so well and she said everything I meant to say," he said, "so that I could do us all a great favor by simply associating myself with her remarks and sitting down.

"I would also like to thank Dr. Anagostopoulos for reminding us of the infamous capacity of faculty members to be contrary with one another," he continued. "Until he said it, I hadn't realized that probably 90 percent of the Congress once were on university faculties."

He went on to introduce all of the dignitaries he had in tow. Special cheers arose when he drawled, "And you have a college here named after one of my great heroes, Thurgood Marshall. I've brought with me his son who works for me in the White House, Thurgood Marshall, Jr. Stand up, Goody!"

Clinton spoke broadly about the ideals of multiculturalism and diversity. "Can we fulfill the promise of America by embracing all our citizens of all races, not just at a university, where people have the benefit of enlightened teachers and the time to think and grow and get to know each other, but in the daily life of every American community?" he asked. In the middle of his speech, immediately before introducing the subject of affirmative action, the president made his most overt statement about our own peculiar problem at UCSD:

> There are no children who, because of their ethnic or racial background, cannot meet the highest academic standards, if we set them and measure our students against them, if we give them well-trained teachers and well-equipped classrooms, and if we continue to support reasoned reforms to achieve excellence like the charter school movement.

A wild cheer and sustained applause broke out, interrupting the progress of his speech. Bud Mehan, who was seated in the faculty section of the audience between two of our fiercest opponents, later told me that one of them gasped aloud.

Published in the *San Diego Union-Tribune*
June 14, 1997 © Dave Kellett

On his way off the stage, Clinton stopped in front of me to give the audience—and more important, the press—a rousing fist in the air as a sign of triumph. This predetermined and staged moment made the front page of newspapers both in the U.S. and in Europe. Several friends living around the world called the next day to say that they saw me with President Clinton not only on the cover of the *New York Times*, but also in *Le Monde*, *Le Figaro*, *El Pais*, and the *London Financial Times*.

The Sunday, June 15, 1997 cover of the *Los Angeles Times*. The caption reads: "President Clinton punctuates his commencement speech at UC San Diego with a rousing gesture."   Photo / Ginna Ferazzi

To his credit, the president was well informed about the events of the week. He made it clear that he supported the UCSD Charter High School effort and hoped that his remarks helped get the project back on track. Privately, I took the opportunity to push my belief with him that public universities were the only American institutions capable of shaping the future of public education. He seemed interested in the notion, but I knew he was preoccupied with a myriad of other issues.

Nearly every paper that carried the President's picture and remarks mentioned the irony of his appearing the same week that the University of California faculty voted down the charter school effort. By the following day, what had been a local and statewide news event was now center-stage in the national and international press. It was widely reported that the prestigious faculty of the University of California supported affirmative action so long as it did not have to occur in their backyard.

President Clinton's visit highlighted the agonizing question of minority participation at the university and put overwhelming pressure on the campus to save the UCSD Charter High School. Some of the UC regents pressured Dynes behind the scenes, especially since the public display of local NIMBY-ism so soon after they eliminated affirmative action made them look particularly heartless. Newspapers and talk shows pilloried the UC faculty and pummeled the chancellor until he initiated an awkward salvation effort during the summer recess.

Death and Transfiguration

Still embittered over Dynes' acceptance of the negative mail ballot, I refused invitations to join the new UCSD Outreach Task Force that was hastily empaneled to reconsider the feasibility of a campus charter school. It made little sense for me to join a new effort to salvage the charter school initiative after having spent the previous four years advocating for the very same solution.

It was clear, however, that the future of the chancellor was inextricably tied to resurrecting an idea that he had allowed to be crucified on an altar called "joint governance." The summer committee's task was to help the faculty save face and pluck an unsteady new chancellor from disaster. In its recovery mission, the joint administration and faculty committee had to somehow make it appear that campus elders had not grievously blundered.

The rescue mission lumbered on all summer with weekly public testimony and faculty senate hearings. The faculty senate insisted that our principal detractors be on the task force as well as a collection of newly-aroused progressives who, up until this point, had conspicuously remained on the sidelines during the fray.

Two important things had changed, however. First, as a result of the heavy lobbying by local UC Regents John Davies and Peter Preuss, the chancellor had finally come out in full unequivocal support of the on-campus charter school. Both regents had been appointed by Governor Wilson and were conservative Republican allies of Ward Connerly, especially in the anti-affirmative action movement. They saw the San Diego effort to open a charter school for poor children as the alternative to affirmative action that had escaped their imagination during the contemptuous debates of 1994-1995.

Davies, who had been a close political advisor to Governor Wilson, saw his support for the UCSD Charter High School as the "political fix" that could innoculate the conservative Republicans from the accusation that they were racists. Preuss, on the other hand, was less motivated by grand political calculations. His ambitions in the enterprise were instinctive and more personal. Although a registered Republican, Peter behaved and discussed issues as someone who was decidedly apolitical. A naturalized German immigrant who had made considerable wealth in technology, he felt deeply the need to give back to a country that had been so good to him. Together, Davies and Preuss, who were essentially Bob Dynes' employers, ordered him to build the charter school as quickly as possible.

The second important change was that Dynes and the academic senate appointed Professors Paul Drake and Nick Spitzer as co-chairs of the summer task force. Drake entered the summer as a successful political scientist whose research spanned Latin America. He had been chair of his department and was now serving as the dean of the social sciences. He impressed everyone he met as the archetypical liberal academic—he often spoke about the social injustices in the world but never could see how he might be able to translate his personal predisposition into professional obligation. Spitzer, on the contrary, was a distinguished biologist who did not necessarily have to confront any loss in translation between the personal and the professional. As he was a scientist, no one expected him to have or understand social compassion, but he did. He was as gregarious as his handlebar moustache was wide.

Unlike a social scientist, who might be considered professionally responsible for solving society's problems, Nick was allowed to blithely assert a social solution and not be held accountable for its success or error. He creatively exploited and enjoyed his ambiguous position and pushed the work of the summer committee forward with an enviable mixture of humor and vigor.

When students returned to campus in September, the Drake/Spitzer committee held public hearings where each speaker championed the idea of a UCSD sponsored charter school. The most memorable was a brilliant set of remarks delivered by Rabbi Lisa Goldstein, director of San Diego Hillel. I could not dispel the feeling that the task force's proceedings were a pantomime performance that had been demanded by the most vulgar sort of public humiliation—theirs and mine.

Meanwhile, the original steering committee continued to meet to monitor the developments of the Drake/Spitzer group. We concluded that we had to hang together in order to make the "new" school proposal remain as true to our original mission as possible. After all, any new proposal might move the school off campus, selectively recruit only high-achieving students, or even admit children of the faculty in an effort to appease the virulent NIMBY-ism that had caused us so much grief. Our resolute, disagreeable presence, we thought, would keep the campus honest as it clawed its way out of the mess in which it found itself.

I was still on sabbatical leave as the fall term began. During a steering committee meeting on the morning of Thursday, October 16, someone ran into the room to tell us that Bill McGill had been taken to the emergency room at Thornton Hospital. It was unclear how serious the situation was, but I knew that the stress of the preceding months had taken a merciless toll on his spirits and body.

It was a restless weekend. Guilt plagued me whenever I called the hospital for an update—I felt like an assailant calling to check on the condition of his victim.

My beloved friend and mentor William McGill died three days later, on a Sunday.

At the eulogy, UC President Richard Atkinson said, "Bill

McGill was one of the major figures in higher education in the period following World War II. He was a superb scientist, distinguished president of two of America's leading universities, and a passionate advocate of university involvement in addressing the challenging issues facing society." These were elegant and true words, but I found no words of my own.

Pat Ledden called that evening sensing my feelings of guilt. "There was nothing you could do, Cecil," he said. Yet, even then, I could find no words.

By November, under the steady and unrelenting eye of statewide politicians and the California media, the faculty had fully reversed itself and approved the fabrication of a new campus entity called the Center for Research in Educational Equity, Assessment, and Teaching Excellence, or "CREATE."

CREATE rudely cobbled together dozens of ongoing student outreach efforts that lined up for additional funding promised by the state legislature. The usual players in the campuswide affirmative action industry were ironically shaking more dollars from the campus that failed to act affirmatively. Those same parties, for the most part, continued their open hostility to the idea of a campus-based charter school for poor children.

However, both clandestine and official equivocation were now moot. Their membership in CREATE meant that they had to support the entire agenda of the new administrative organization or else they would not get their share of the affirmative action guilt money now spilling towards every UC campus. CREATE was charged to build the charter school as the centerpiece of its existence, but in fact it was its *raison d'etre*.

By now, the campus had established a checkered history of voting on the charter school. The faculty, through the representative assembly, had voted in favor by a two-to-one majority on May 6th; then they had rejected the proposal in a mail ballot of the entire faculty by a slim majority a month later; and now, following the frantic pace of the 19-member summer committee headed by Drake and Spitzer, they had endorsed the charter school once again in the UCSD Representative Assembly by a 58-5 vote. Although five members of the representative assembly failed to appreciate the tortured necessity of approving the UCSD Charter High School, the mail ballot was overturned and we now had a green light to move forward. The proposal, however, no longer called for only a high school, but for an even larger and more extensive secondary school, grades 6-12.

The local press remained distrustful and maintained its relentless pressure on the campus to build the charter school. The day after the November 25, 1997 vote approving the school in the representative assembly (again), the *San Diego Union-Tribune* was cautiously optimistic. A staff editorial titled "Back on Track" commented:

> **UCSD Panel Gives Green Light to Charter School**
>
> We would like to herald Tuesday's decisive vote by the UCSD faculty panel to press onward toward establishing a campus-based charter school as proof that the professors are solidly behind this worthy project. And the sense we get from the vote and related comments is that Chancellor Robert Dynes' optimism is well-founded and he should indeed commence raising funds for the experimental school.
>
> Then again, we keep remembering how the charter school was blind-sided last spring when the faculty narrowly voted in a mail ballot against the plan. Could history repeat itself this time in light of lingering opposition to the school? Our guess is that it will not, because Dynes and other charter school proponents took care to build a fair amount of consensus among faculty members who were lukewarm about the project.

The article went on to single out Paul Drake and Nick Spitzer for their leadership in building a positive faculty consensus despite the paper's lingering trepidation and perception of UCSD elitism.

The progressive visions of Gilman and Kerr now echoed from the editorial pages of a conservative newspaper. I felt that the late Thurgood Marshall, too, through the college named in his honor, continued to be an agent of change, who now compelled the University of California, a multi-billion dollar educational corporation, to reassume its nineteenth century land-grant role in changing the normal order of things on behalf of the state's ignored citizens. Chancellor Dynes had refused to accept my resignation, but had instead approved a sabbatical leave. With the favorable turn of events, I returned to my post as provost to participate in the development of the project.

If there was residual faculty bitterness about having to build a charter school on campus, it remained hidden behind frozen smiles and self-congratulatory statements of accomplishment. The existence of CREATE provided the institutional camouflage for the faculty to approve the establishment of the charter school as one submerged element of general campus outreach. The charter school, however, was the only element of CREATE that was new.

CREATE's mission statement struck all of the familiar notes of our initial challenge. Its five structural prongs: Evaluation, Research, Outreach & Recruitment, Teacher Education, and K-12 Clusters, each radiated from something called the "Model School." All except the last item were a re-patching of ongoing entrepreneurial and educational programs already in operation on campus.

Except for the pre-existing Teacher Education Program that Bud directed, all elements of CREATE were totally reliant upon soft money coming from the UC Office of the President and the California legislature. Essentially, this new organization was a freebee, wholly unsupported by campus resources. The faculty eventually endorsed the idea, but it served only as a cover to rescue the new chancellor and campus pride from the scorn of politicians, the press, and the community.

Chancellor Dynes found just the right person for the unenviable task of reviving the "dead" charter school project. Peter Gourevitch, an experienced faculty member, political science department chair, and founding dean of the School of International Relations and Pacific Studies, had earned a well-deserved reputation as a "fixer" on campus. He and I had been chairs of our respective departments during the same period in the 1980's and were much discussed then, as he was being recruited to Cornell and I to Dartmouth.

Peter convinced me that I had to come in from out of the cold, and I agreed to co-direct the planning effort with him. He was tasked to put the charter school plans back together and, in part, to be my minder. Together, we spent the next 18 months resuscitating the basic concepts of the original proposal, and I found in him another warrior who truly believed in the school.

Once the campus decision to establish CREATE had been finalized, more of the liberal establishment that had watched the fray from the sidelines began to emerge. Progressives of all sorts joined committees and worked tirelessly to bring the charter school to fruition. Their sudden interest in outreach was curiously late, but welcome.

Peter displayed the skills of a master strategist and the patience of a stone. He was less abrasive than I and possessed the emotional detachment to sit through withering hours of meetings with reformed foes whose tortured compliance continued to make my stomach turn. He had been a member of the Drake/Spitzer task force and was ready to collate that group's new language with the spirit and mission of the original Charter School Steering Committee's proposal.

The campus and chancellor were now fully engaged in resurrecting the charter school idea. For the first time, the chancellor no longer felt politically compelled to include the vocal opponents of the charter school in the decision making.

It had been a long and bitter campaign, but we had arrived. The school was going to be built. However odious I might have found past hypocrisy, our public university was now going to act on its democratic principles and build the first urban Educational Field Station.

I only wished that Bill had lived to see it.

Dr. William McGill and the author.
Photo © Camera's Eye 1997

Chapter Six

Preuss School UCSD

The new charter school proposal was drawn directly from the old one. With the battle for campus approval behind us, we began to move on three fronts off the campus. Throughout the entire skirmish at UCSD, we had held only tenuous talks with representatives of San Diego city schools. With campus approval, we now needed to start negotiations with the local school district on funding levels, matters of legal liability, transportation, and the operating budget. Although the publicly elected members of the San Diego School Board were overwhelmingly supportive of UCSD's newfound courage to proceed, the mid-level staff of the school district's legal and financial departments were less than encouraging.

Brave New World

In preparation for submitting the revised proposal, Peter Gourevitch and I spent time visiting with each member of the school board individually. The members had read the draft proposal and told us that they were unaware of any staff opposition. Their uniform opinion was that the UCSD proposal to establish a charter school would meet with staff approval and garner an affirmative vote.

The school district's legal staff, however, threw up one obstacle after another. After just a few meetings, Peter and I became convinced that we should bring in UC General Counsel Anne Parode to stand toe-to-toe with them. Quickly, all of their objections melted away and revealed an institutional culture that abhorred change of any kind. The dreary hallways of the San Diego Unified School District's building on Normal Street belied an even drearier sloth, devoted to making sure that nothing new ever happened.

Like many public school districts, San Diego had been threatened and sued more times than anyone wanted to remember. Coupled with the historic pounding that its educators had received from both the public and politicians for school failures, the net result was the entrenchment of a culture characterized by an attitude of "can't do, won't try!" The district's financial department also had substantial worries caused by years of budget reversals and shortfalls. Both worked in tandem to frustrate our efforts and try to drive us away.

I had originally initiated discussions with the outgoing superintendent of the San Diego city schools as early as 1995. But it was clear that, on the advice of her staff, Dr. Bertha Pendleton did not want to leave office with a raging conflagration between the district and the University of California. During the weeks that we wound our way through the hallways to meet with the members of the school board, Alan Bersin was preparing to become the new superintendent of the San Diego Unified School District. Bersin had been United States Attorney for the Southern District of California and responsible for federal law and immigration enforcement along a 180-mile stretch of the U.S./Mexico border. As the chief of "la Migra," he was immediately viewed with suspicion by most of the Latino community, a community that contributed over half of the school age children in San Diego.

Bersin was a controversial figure from the beginning. This was not only because of his recent background in border law enforcement, but because of a testy personality that seemed to alienate nearly everyone with whom he came into contact. When he assumed the post of superintendent on July 1, 1998, we were within weeks of submitting the UCSD Charter School proposal to the school district for final approval. He, however, wanted more time to adjust to the office before being confronted with our controversial proposal.

Campus opinion was divided: Some thought that he was a Yale University Brahmin with strong connections to his former law school classmate who occupied the White House at the time. Others, including me, simply thought that his tough nature belied a deeper lack of confidence—making him appear socially awkward. Bersin implored Peter and me to delay submitting the proposal, but the urgency of the final campus vote and our newfound momentum made that impossible. We decided to obey the pace of events taking place on the campus and push towards submitting the proposal for a vote by the San Diego School Board as quickly as possible.

During the early stages of the charter school proposal in 1996, meetings with representatives of the local teachers' association did not go well. I had reviewed with them the portions of the California charter school legislation that allowed an entity to put forward a proposal to essentially subcontract with the local school district to run a specific school, utilizing the share of funds that would normally be spent at the students' home school sites. They seemed to accept our three admissions criteria of low income, first in family, and motivation to excel in a college preparatory environment.

Their true worry was that we would indeed be successful, and put pressure on them and the district to improve all schools in a similar manner. This less than sanguine notion, however, was often hidden behind warnings of a less amicable upheaval if we did not accept the union agreement already in place with the district. I reminded them that charter school legislation did not require that we or any other entity do so, and that we would apply UC staff hiring and grievance policies and procedures for all credentialed teachers and staff at our charter school.

My assurances did not mollify the union reps because it meant that they could not exert hiring and curricular controls over our school. At each encounter, I made it clear that UCSD would not accept the collective bargaining agreement into the functions of our school. Nothing had changed by the time Peter and I met with them in early 1998. Each meeting ended cordially, and the labor representatives declared that they would not publicly oppose UCSD's effort to open a charter school on its campus. Nevertheless, they made no such promise about their continuing private opposition.

At the time, California legislation required that independent petitioners for a charter school seek endorsement from at least 20% of the teaching staff at a standing school. As Rafael, Bud, and I went around to local elementary and middle schools seeking such endorsements, we often found that the teachers' union had peppered mailboxes in advance with warnings not to sign our petition. At each meeting, there was usually at least one spokesperson arguing against our effort.

One of the oddest encounters occurred at Keiller Middle School. While the teachers were friendly, one gentleman in the back of the room spoke vociferously in opposition, suggesting the possibility of several dire consequences for public education if teachers signed our charter school proposal. By the end of the meeting, all of the teachers present had signed our petition—except him. We must have been convincing, though, because the same fellow met me at my car asking to sign the petition after all. He said that he had to publicly speak against our enterprise, but he personally agreed with our plan and wanted to know if we might have a position for him at the UCSD Charter School.

Such was the curious trail of organizations and individuals we had to circumnavigate as we pressed forward.

Following his stint as my intern, Andrew Sutherland had worked for a year as the "project coordinator" for the charter school with funding coming from the grant he won from the UC Regents. His curious status as both a UCSD student and an employee of the UC Regents had allowed him to play to different strengths. That fall, once it had become clear that the campus would build the school, he left to pursue a Ph.D. at SUNY Buffalo.

Consequently, I turned to John Lien, my newest intern, who had spoken so elegantly the night we won our first representative assembly vote, to coordinate information sessions with parents at elementary and middle schools in the city. We met in the evenings with school PTA organizations and parent groups to inform them of the 1999 opening of the UCSD Charter School. Parents and elementary school teachers never failed to respond enthusiastically.

John also set to work on a draft for the school's entrance application. Bud, in his role as director of UCSD's Teacher Education Program, handled the rewriting of the proposal. Within six months, we had negotiated the budget with the school district, secured university land for the school, and hired HMC Architects to design the building.

In June of 1998, Chancellor Dynes and members of the planning committee formally presented the UCSD proposal to establish the charter school at a public meeting of the San Diego School Board. The elected members, despite the continued grumbling of district staff, unanimously approved it.

What's in a Name?

Peter Preuss, throughout this entire tortured effort, had been actively lobbying behind the scene for the establishment of the charter school. However, during legislative confirmation hearings for his appointment to the Board of Regents of the University of California, Peter openly expressed his dislike for the affirmative action admissions policy at UC campuses. Despite our disagreement on that issue, I testified before the California Senate endorsing his appointment.

Preuss' position was complex and nuanced. We had first met at a black tie event in 1984 when we shared joint honors: he was chosen UCSD Alumni of the Year, and I was given the UCSD Teaching Excellence Award. Throughout the evening, we talked about education, and he spoke passionately about wanting to "give back" to the community and country that had made him a wealthy software mogul.

He displayed an honest and infectious belief in the promise America has to offer a recent immigrant, and I believed that he truly meant it. While we were searching for a principal for our emerging charter school, Peter and Peggy Preuss confirmed their first pledge of $500,000 and announced a new $5,000,000 gift towards the capital campaign.

Their enthusiasm was so high, in fact, that Peter and Peggy went on to actively participate in raising the remaining $9,000,000 for the new facility. In the end, six major donors came forward with one million dollars each. Several mid-range donations from local individuals completed the fundraising effort with unusual speed.

Peter and Peggy Preuss
Photo / Melissa Jacobs

Meanwhile, HMC Architects busily created renderings for a building design that was borne out of Building Advisory Committee discussions that stipulated the need for physical separation between the middle school and the high school; outdoor spaces where tutoring and mentoring would take place under supervision; and placement on campus within walking distance of the Geisel Library.

The pace of events turned typical planning protocols on their heads. After the Preuss' initial capital campaign donation, the architects were let loose to design without concern for budget limits, and we agreed early on that we would employ a "design/build" strategy. This meant that the campus would commence building based on the wet blueprints as they became available while the designers scurried to complete the remaining drawings. All the while, we continued to plumb the community to raise the remaining funding for the rapidly rising building.

Even as the contractors were digging holes along wiggly chalk lines drawn on an 8.1 acre site on campus, we were still negotiating with school district staff about the annual operating budget. At the time, charter schools were barely a five-year-old phenomenon that had overwhelmed public school staff and policy makers. Our crude calculations suggested that we could expect per capita funding of around $5,800 per student, plus categorical allocations that typically target low-income students and families. Among the latter budget options were resources for second language acquisition, free or reduced-cost lunch subsidy, funding for after-school programs, and other support mechanisms available to schools serving large numbers of children needing specialized help.

Peter Gourevitch and I were in over our heads in dealing with the school district's budget sharpies and legal hawks. So, we called for help from UCSD Resource Management's professional staff, who were more accustomed to creating and handling budget outlays. They were our "green eyeshade" folks, and they were magnificent.

UCSD's Judi O'Boyle headed the capital planning and also oversaw the design and construction for what we would eventually name Preuss School UCSD. She worked closely with the architects and the prime contractor in keeping the project on schedule. I drove by the site every day, including weekends. During the early construction, Judi was often seen standing ankle-deep in mud holding a chart or blueprint over her head and staring across a sea of dismembered two-by-fours, pointing towards what was to become the school library. A few weeks later, she would be wearing a listing hardhat and jabbing a ballpoint pen in the direction of the future playing fields.

Sylvia Lepe, another UCSD staffer, seemed too young to take on the state and school district's barracuda bureaucrats. By our third or fourth weekly meeting with district staff, however, she had prepared an outline of *their* overall annual budget profile and an explanation of how the district could fully fund the children of Preuss School UCSD.

Now we were flying with the wind. Numerous other professional staff at UCSD began to step forward to contribute their particular expertise. Larry Barrett, director of Housing and Dining Services, helped develop the lunch room facility; Jack Hug, director of Physical Plant Services, came forward with plans for handling janitorial and landscape services; Greg Snee, director of Transportation & Parking Services, changed campus plans for parking lots and re-routed a street to make more room for the playground; techie Jim Valetta led the design of the school's internet services; and Sherman George, the Media Center's director, designed the audio/video support systems for the classrooms and multipurpose center (while also providing much of the benevolent and sarcastic wit that kept everyone in good humor).

Perhaps more significantly, the campus' janitorial crew, hospital orderlies, groundskeepers, carpenters, electricians, and mail carriers slowed their pace and smiled with pride and curiosity when they passed the giant hole in the ground that would soon become our school. For the first time in its history, the university along Gilman Drive had become a village as everyone contributed to the start of this unique undertaking.

Bob Dynes made it clear that the Preuss School had to open in the fall of 1999, with or without a building. We were a year from that opening date and just starting to hire a school director. The grant that Andrew had secured a year earlier was running out and we had no real sketch of the curriculum or the teachers to be hired. UCSD Risk Management had to determine an acceptable level of liability options in the running of a public charter school on the campus. Housing and Dining Services had to negotiate with their counterparts at the school district on appropriate lunch menus. Transportation Services had to run traffic studies on the impact of fifteen buses lining up along Voigt Drive five years hence, at full enrollment, to load and unload eight hundred students twice a day. Nevertheless, all of us monitored the favorable swing in public opinion towards UCSD as this unique project gained momentum.

At Thurgood Marshall College, Rafael Hernandez led an initiative to place UCSD tutors at the Preuss School and taught a class in UCSD's Teacher Education Program for this purpose.

While Bud was being drawn more and more into the burgeoning activities of CREATE, Pat Ledden returned to his patrician ways and assumed an even greater role as my counselor and wise confidant in the endeavor.

The Leader

That summer, we initiated a nationwide search for an academic leader to serve as the founding director of Preuss School UCSD. The search garnered more than one hundred and thirty applicants, several from San Diego. The local candidates were known to us and were admired principals at local San Diego high schools. The search committee included UCSD faculty and staff as well as several leaders from area public schools. Our objective was to find and appoint someone who had high academic standards and extensive experience working with the children and families attending inner-city schools.

I flew to Tucson to meet with one of our finalists. She was the principal at a high school that had been troubled the previous year by violent race riots between African American and Latino students. It had been a typical encounter where kids in a changing neighborhood were pitted against one another for limited jobs, welfare, housing, and attention. She had been sent in not only to restore order, but to raise the scholastic achievement of a school in academic freefall. Our candidate had installed a new campus-wide college-prep curriculum and, in two short years, was showing remarkable progress.

I found her to be an ambitious, strong young leader and the possessor of a clear vision for achieving academic goals. We learned that she had been raised in a loving family of migrant workers in California's Central Valley and instinctively understood the difficult lives our students would bring into the classroom. Our only doubt was that the Tucson appointment was her first leadership post and, although successful in this relatively short period of time, there was not a track record of sustained progress that could be measured. Although I had doubts, she was my sentimental favorite.

Doris Alvarez, on the other hand, was a well-known and well-respected principal at one of the most challenging high schools in San Diego. A year earlier, she was named Principal of the Year by the National Association of Secondary Schools and was presented the award by President Bill Clinton at the White House. She was the most experienced of our three finalists with a teaching career that began in 1964. She began in counseling and went on to distinguished service as a vice principal and then a principal in area schools with large enrollments of low-income students. Along the way, she had earned a doctorate in educational counseling. By the time of her interview with us, she had been principal at San Diego's Hoover High School for ten years.

Hoover High had undergone significant transformations under her watch. When I first met Doris, Hoover had an enrollment of mostly low-income African American and Latino students. By 1998, the student population included many newly arrived children of immigrants from Somalia, Ethiopia, the former Soviet Union, and Eastern Europe. The hallways of Hoover rang with voices speaking over forty-three languages.

The questioning of the final candidates was friendly, but tough and earnest as well. We knew that the founding director of this school had to demonstrate that he or she was a first-rate academic leader with strong values. This person also had to be capable of functioning well in a charter school independent of typical school district authority. Perhaps most important, our choice had to be comfortable operating a secondary school on a university campus that demanded a great deal in terms of performance and academic excellence. The challenges we set for our urban Educational Field Station were great, but so would be the benefits if we were successful.

Despite our confidence in the overall project, we knew that the director would be the key to success. The director had to be a dreamer whose eyes were wide open, a person of vision who also understood the anguished past and troubled present of our precious students. The director had to be part educator and part shaman, rabbi, priest, and pastor. That person would also have to know how to manage the intense public scrutiny our unique school would endure. But above all, the director would have to be a confident academic leader who instinctively understood Bill McGill's faith in education as the common leveler. Dr. Doris Alvarez was that person.

While the opportunity to be the founding director of this unique school had attracted a wide variety of personalities, including several who touted the latest interests in technology and curricular reform, it was our opinion that we needed a school head who held strong traditional educational values and not someone interested in using these youngsters as their innovative experiment. Our urban Educational Field Station was to be a demonstration model for best practices, not a laboratory for innovation for innovation's sake. Doris was known as a demanding educational leader with high educational standards and a task-oriented demeanor. Although I had doubts about her blunt style, she was the best person for our novel enterprise.

Even before the official start of her appointment, Alvarez quickly began to put together a teaching and administrative staff. Her first selection was Ms. Jan Gabay, San Diego County Teacher of the Year for 1986. Carol Sobek was head counselor at Hoover High School and assumed the same role at the Preuss School. As Alvarez began the task of filling in the details of opening and running a new school, our level of interaction increased rapidly.

The chancellor appointed me to chair a board of directors to set the policy and procedures for the school. Doris and I tacitly agreed that she would look after everything inside the walls, and that the Preuss School Board of Directors would essentially take care of the more omnibus matters outside the walls.

The eighteen-month construction period began relatively smoothly, and the groundbreaking ceremony for the new school was a major event. Dynes was the hero of the day, as he had staked his chancellorship and legacy in reversing faculty sentiment. Silver shovels were plied by him and a small collection of primary school children we recruited to turn the soil to warm applause. Peter Preuss addressed the outdoor audience about his duty to give back to society in meaningful ways. In another context, these remarks might have seemed vainglorious, but on this day, the repetition of his personal story rang true.

With construction of the official home of the school going forward, we opened Preuss School UCSD on September 11, 1999, on the campus of Thurgood Marshall College. The Thurgood Marshall College Student Council agreed to temporarily vacate their student services and lunchroom areas to make room for the first 150 students. The project also required that we rent and renovate three temporary bungalows for the counseling staff and for an extra classroom. These were inelegant spaces, but the tight fit overlooked the magnificent UCSD Geisel Library and a scenic grove of eucalyptus trees facing UCSD's Price Center. Fortunately, it doesn't rain often in San Diego, but the occasional downpour turned the walking paths between the buildings into small cascading deltas and ravines.

Despite primitive beginnings, however, morale was high among the school's teaching staff, and students seemed mesmerized by their surroundings on the UCSD campus.

Nevertheless, there were a few troubling aspects to Preuss School's opening. When UCSD announced that Doris Alvarez was to be the director of this auspicious undertaking, I received several telephone calls from local preachers and politicians in San Diego's African American community lamenting the appointment. A few years earlier, some African American parents had tangled with Doris over the progress of their children at Hoover High School. They had enlisted the aid of local leaders in accusing her of disregarding the concerns of the black community. The dispute made the newspapers, but amounted to little more than a passing skirmish and faded from the papers as the 2000 election year came into focus.

Much of that first year required a period of adjustment for

all. Doris had to settle into both the liberty and the confines of running a secondary charter school on a research university campus. Students, especially the 8th grade children, had to endure the uncustomary imposition of a rigorous, grade-appropriate curriculum. And parents had to become comfortable with the idea that UCSD, not the local school district, was running this secondary school in the high academic terms associated with the University of California.

It Don't Mean a Thing

Our proposal called for the admission of students in a controlled manner. In order to be financially viable, however, it was necessary that enrollments grow quickly. In September of 1999, we opened with 150 students and ten teachers, evenly divided among grades six, seven, and eight. The following academic year, Preuss School would add a new 6th grade and additional students in 7th, 8th, and 9th grades, growing by nearly 300% to 430 students and twenty-five teachers. CREATE's first report on the development of the Preuss School tracked our management of enrollments.

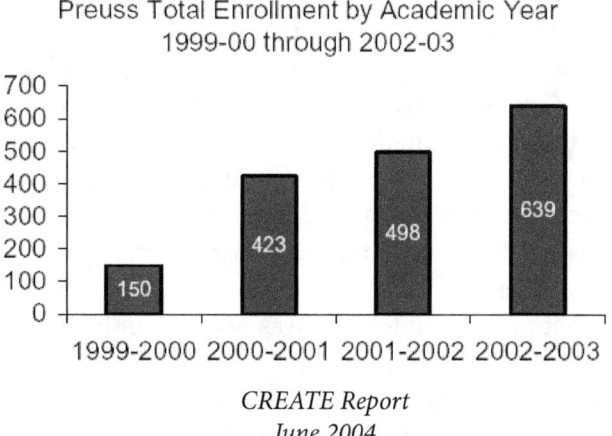

CREATE Report
June 2004

Although we realized that growth was important for financial and social viability, we were also cognizant of the challenges of combining middle school children with the bigger kids who would inhabit the high school grades. It was, therefore, also important to grow at an even pace among the various grades for an even distribution between grades 6-8 and 9-12.

In order to properly prepare the 8th grade students for UC competitive eligibility within five years, it was necessary to immediately introduce them to a college preparatory curriculum, ready or not. We consequently directed many of the enrichment supports to their adjustment. This included small class sizes, university tutors in the classroom, and longer time on task. The school day for all of the first-year students began at 8:30 A.M. and ended late in the afternoon. Saturday morning classes were available for additional instruction, and the school year was 11 months in duration.

The first assessments of our students' progress compared with cohort groups not attending Preuss School came at the end of the first complete year, when all 150 students took the national standardized tests. The results were impressive, although mixed.

The grade-level tests were given in language arts, reading, and math. Our fifty sixth-graders entered at the 63rd percentile in math prior to attending Preuss and now registered an 82nd percentile average at the end of the first year. Indeed, all grades showed marked improvement on all standardized testing areas after one year, with the exception of the 8th graders, who registered a thirteen-percent decrease on the math tests.

Their decreased math score was alarming because math is one of the barrier areas that often prohibits progress towards successful acceptance to college. Doris felt that the decrease in math scores was due to the fact that the 8th-grade curriculum was far above the students' level of preparation in prior years. She also thought that their math teacher was not responding to the challenge of the school as she had wished. The older 8th graders had been in low-achieving schools longer than the students in the lower grades and their progress was stunted by systematic miseducation. While we were encouraged by the overall progress, we knew that the trend in math had to be reversed quickly.

We were wary of relying too heavily on test scores. Debate continued about the value of using standardized test scores to judge academic success. After only one year of operation, however, those scores were one measure used to capture a snapshot of how our students were progressing, relative to their prior history. We were equally wary about making comparisons with district schools on these same measures. Despite our reservations, John Lien developed a chart showing Preuss School UCSD scores compared with scores of these grade levels in the wider district:

GRADE LEVEL	LANGUAGE TESTS	READING TESTS	MATH TESTS
6th	63% prior to Preuss	52% prior to Preuss	63% prior to Preuss
	68% end of 1st year	74% end of 1st year	82% end of 1st year
	+8% change	+42% change	+30% change
7th	66% prior to Preuss	64% prior to Preuss	68% prior to Preuss
	80% end of 1st year	74% end of 1st year	72% end of 1st year
	+21% change	+15% change	+6% change
8th	63% prior to Preuss	61% prior to Preuss	64% prior to Preuss
	71% end of 1st year	64% end of 1st year	56% end of 1st year
	+13% change	+5% change	-13% change

John Lien's Report
June 2004

This study proved somewhat useful as an early indicator of student progress. The problem, though, with his measurement was that the students were self-selected from a pool of highly motivated parents and students who understood that they were participants in a high-expectations environment. I could not help but find the comparison encouraging, however.

While we academics scratched our heads over the numbers, both Peter and Peggy Preuss were regular visitors at the school's temporary site. It was hard for them to stay away from their new progeny. It was also hard for me to stay away from the small colony of buildings that housed my dream. Throughout the day, I could see from my office window at Thurgood Marshall College the commotion of pre-teens and teenagers scurrying between the buildings during class changes. The parents and children had trusted us to conduct an adventure on their behalf that was essentially untested. Perhaps because the Preuss School was under the auspices of the University of California, San Diego, the project was accorded a degree of public trust that we perhaps had not yet earned.

We continued to work on two fronts during that first year: teaching the first admits of the school, grades 6-8, in temporary facilities on the Thurgood Marshall College campus, and pushing forward to finish the new building on the eastern edge of the campus. As bricks and mortar were delivered to the site, the campus was heavily involved in raising funds for the new building's completion. The Preuss family hosted several parties at which we made appeals for support. The long and critical media attention of the past three years was beginning to pay off. Everyone in attendance at these parties knew the tortured history of our journey to this point and came to the aid of the project.

Parents of the youngsters were regular visitors at the school and often shadowed the buses to the site, remaining at a distance as their children, wearing new Preuss School uniforms, scurried into makeshift classrooms. During that unusually rainy fall season, they sometimes lingered in the eucalyptus grove on the fringe of the school site, peering from around the trees in wonder and expectation at the gentle commotion taking place. During the first parent meetings, they were full of questions aimed more at determining our resolve and character than at understanding the curriculum. Were we to be trusted? Would their children be safe among the complex bustle of a mysterious institution? The parents were willing to trust UCSD to perform a miracle in their lives and the lives of their children. Nonetheless, they were cautious—and with good reason.

UCSD was an alien environment to them. They knew that it was a place inhabited by a lot of smart people who were mostly white. Would their children be accepted, cared for, and left alone to study and learn? Their trepidation was palpable and justified. Throughout the forty-year existence of the La Jolla campus, we had not shown much evidence of being truly concerned with the welfare of families south of Interstate 8 [where a major freeway physically separates the traditionally African American and Hispanic neighborhoods from the rest of the city]. Truth be told, I shared their worries.

Each day, hundreds of UCSD students passed the new community of young scholars in their midst with great curiosity. The opening of the school was front-page news, and many took time from chattering on their cell phones to gawk and wonder. Although half a decade would pass before the 8th graders would graduate from high school, it's hard to appreciate just what was going on in the heads of those first Preuss School students as the San Diego version of winter came and went and we leaned towards the opening of the new facility across campus the following September.

As the first academic year of Preuss School UCSD came to a close, we were still haggling with the San Diego city school district about the continued level of annual funding when its staff introduced yet another stumbling block to derail the project.

District staff were now demanding that we eliminate all student eligibility criteria and accept any child presented for admission. This would have been a two-fold disaster. The elimination of eligibility criteria as described would result in multiple applications from the children of wealthy La Jolla families. Second, it would force the admission of students from all over the city who had no intention of pursuing a rigorous college prep curriculum.

We engaged in a long exchange of memos, but eventually ceased communication on this issue as their position was in violation of California's charter school legislation and did not enjoy the support of their bosses, the elected board members of the San Diego Unified School District. Throughout all of the backroom turbulence, Superintendent Alan Bersin remained silent, choosing not to endorse, condemn, or even recognize the existence of the

Preuss School UCSD.

The Preuss School's board of directors, appointed by Chancellor Dynes, functioned well during the first year, successfully confronting legal issues and construction details, fundraising, and assisting the director. As part of the deal authorizing the establishment of the Preuss School, the UCSD Academic Senate required a specified number of faculty to be permanent members of the board. Although this negotiated provision was regulatory in intent, certain faculty members began to emerge as true leaders, making serious and important contributions.

Julian Betts joined the board as a young economist trained in the austere intellectual realm of econometrics. His work dealt with the measurement of various educational reforms as they contribute to determining lifelong income. His elegant quantitative studies soon proved a meaningful counterbalance to my overly optimistic inclinations. He gently forced me and the entire enterprise to carefully scrutinize all aspects of the governance of the school. In particular, Julian scrupulously followed the selection of student applicants placed into the lottery for admissions. At his urging, all admitted applicants were to be followed as part of the overall denominator when judging student progress. Having Julian in the room at the board's monthly meetings forced us all to prove our passions and test our intentions.

Peter Gourevitch proved a consummate strategist in gaming out encounters between our charter school and the local authorities. He continued to be my minder for a while, but eventually led our relationship towards a fully participatory collaboration. Like me, he would soon lose his beloved wife, Lisa Hirschman, to cancer. He and his two boys set up a foundation in her memory to provide psychological counseling to Preuss School students and families in need. His involvement with the Preuss School and the Hirschman Fund allowed him to productively channel and transform his sorrow into helping others. We leaned together in creative grief to nurture the development of the Preuss School UCSD.

Bud Mehan had in the meantime become Director of CREATE and joked that he was now, "the Creator." It was his model of educational scaffolding that framed the curricular, pedagogic, and academic support mechanisms of the Preuss School. He attended all meetings, but was preoccupied with the machinations of the newly formed outreach organization. CREATE had received the lion's share of student outreach funds from the UC Office of the President, and Bud was hiring numerous staff to help shape a series of academic partnerships with several local secondary schools in the inner city.

During the summer of 2000, the school made the move into the new building on the eastern side of the campus. New computers, desks, books, and chairs arrived almost daily as contractors swept up debris and put the finishing touches on the Walton Center and office complex. Bob Dynes showed up on opening day to move chairs and greet parents as they arrived. He was there to shake the hand of every student as he or she got off one of the four yellow school buses in the parking lot. With the long and bitter campaign behind us, he grinned now like a proud papa.

By instinct, Bob Dynes was a progressive and always wanted to do the right thing. He had come to UCSD directly from private industry and worked conscientiously to become a model faculty member. He had talked former NASA astronaut and UCSD physics professor Sally Ride, the first woman in space, into teaching Physics 1 with him. Soon thereafter, he became the chair of his department and then vice chancellor for academic affairs. All the while, he endeavored to understand the faculty and to function successfully as one of them. That desire was his greatest asset and his greatest liability. During our fight for the charter school, he seemed to believe that the strenuous objection of a few faculty opponents was sufficient cause not to proceed. Gaining his footing and a better sense of what it meant to be an academic leader seemed to come later, perhaps as a result of his trial in the matter of the charter school. His challenge was one of wedding his admirable personal instincts with his sense of professional obligation to the university. The task is typical in leadership; especially for someone taking the reins of an idealistic institution like a public university. The opening of the Preuss School had been a crucible for both of us.

Establishing Preuss School UCSD was, in fact, a defining moment for the young campus. No other campus in the UC system could have created such a monument to high academic achievement and to social responsibility. The campus' youth allowed the expression of new ideas and solutions to old problems. Several generations of academics had not yet calcified the institutional rituals or vision of what a public university should be. The campus had opened a new department, college, or school almost every year since 1965. Debate was our currency and creative approaches were mother's milk to a campus seeking to distinguish itself from the older flagship UC. The Preuss School UCSD was now part of that rampant exuberant youthfulness.

As the Preuss School settled into the new building and its second year of operation in September of 2000, a new controversy emerged from within. Students and parents chafed at the constant written and spoken references to their low-income status. Although our target population was, indeed, low-income families, Doris made sure that the Preuss School application stated: "All students must meet the federal school guidelines for economic support known as 'Title One' or the 'Free or Reduced-Priced Meals Program.'" However, newspaper articles that followed the progress of the charter school continually referenced "poor students" or used terms like "poverty" and "disadvantaged" to describe their status and eligibility.

One of the first editions of the student newspaper, the *Preuss Insider*, contained student editorials condemning an article that appeared in a January issue of *Time Magazine* that referred to the students as "poor minorities." Along with student articles in both Spanish and English covering: Vicente Fox, the new president of Mexico; the America's Cup; the governor's recent *State of the State* address; Dr. Martin Luther King, Jr.; and, the Chinese Year of the Snake, an eighth-grader addressed the issue of how the students wanted to be represented:

> Even though the Preuss School's publication class is just starting to learn good writing skills, we are also learning cor-

rect term use and how to refrain from offending anyone who might read our articles.

The author of an article titled, "Build It Yourself," published in the January 8, 2001 issue of *Time* magazine was not aware of the people it may have offended. Many Preuss students were offended by this article, which included the following statements: "The school opened in fall 1999 with 150 6th-8th graders, all of whom are poor enough to qualify for subsidized lunches," and "The University looked to recruit minority students."

This is offensive to many Preuss School students because as Claudia Guerrero said, "some people just don't like being called poor." Also, even though "minority" is not an offensive word, Being called "minority students" is inaccurate.

Yes, not having a lot of money is a requirement for admissions to the Preuss School, but it could have been worded differently, like "low-income" instead of "poor..."

In the magazine article it also states that we are economically underprivileged. Isn't the whole purpose of this school to help kids learn more and to put them ahead?

Time is a great magazine that is filled with facts and information for all ages. This article was most likely not meant to be taken the wrong way. *Time* magazine just didn't think of the way we would feel towards this article.

There are three ways we can solve this problem: we can write letters to *Time* magazine telling them how we feel, we can write letters demanding an apology, or we can drop it. Which one do you think we should do?

The *Time* magazine article was part of a special report dedicated to education reform. It was complimentary and presented the University of California, San Diego as daring and highly innovative. But it was also a national venue that hurt the feelings of the last people on earth that we wanted to see compromised. Doris told me of student lunchtime chatter about the media's continual reference to them as "poor." The disturbance never fully surfaced as an official complaint, but teachers had heard student objections about how they were constantly being described.

I was invited to a Saturday morning meeting of the Parents' Council to address the issue head-on. The parents were divided over the issue; some expressed the students' outrage, others took a peculiar pride in the characterization. Interestingly, it seemed to me that the African American parents (mostly young mothers) objected the most. Just as interesting, it appeared that the Latino mothers were more defiant and proud of what they were accomplishing in the face of the seemingly negative media characterization. Other parents remained aloof from the discussion.

Months later, I came to better understand the sagacious approach of the students. Perhaps because they were appreciative of the leaders who had created this special opportunity for them, they did not openly criticize Doris or me for printing the offending language in school literature and public statements. Rather, they made good use of this national article to express their general outrage at a distant and remote abuser.

The controversy did, however, illuminate a provocative discourse about the nature of disadvantage in this country, in all of its forms. Surrounded by ubiquitous daily reminders that equate money with moral and social rectitude, the students correctly perceived that statements about their economic condition conveyed a greater and more damning connotation about their personal character and ethical potential. Although the students recognized and appreciated the university's effort on their behalf, they flinched at the social baggage often associated with our noble effort.

We got the message. From that point on, all of the media materials we controlled made "off the record" comments advising the avoidance of compromising and offending references. Although we could not control what newspapers chose to print, we promised the parents and students that we would make every effort to caution writers about the controversy. Everyone involved with the Preuss School agreed that we had no intention of changing our income eligibility requirement. Rather, we turned the challenge into an opportunity. At a later meeting of the Parents' Council, I asked the parents to discuss the issue with their families and propose alternative language that we would send to the media for all subsequent publications. They wrestled with the matter for months and we eventually agreed to return to language used in the original 1996 charter school proposal that highlighted the school's similarity with the well-known AVID program in California schools.

It was an imperfect solution. The ongoing discussion, however, brought the members of the Preuss School community closer together. Perhaps the best result was the wholesale realization that we all had to hang together despite absent-minded public assaults on our collective integrity.

Some assaults were more direct. The district's legal staff was never comfortable with charter schools. By the time of our opening, there were fourteen charter schools approved by the San Diego Unified School District and in various stages of operation. Most were charismatic small-scale projects run by churches, community organizations, and teacher/parent collaborations with little administrative experience. The freedom inherent in charter school legislation often led to poor operations and financial mismanagement. Wanting to get a handle on these disparate charter schools, the district sought to create a "single-size-fits-all" approach to the governance structure for all of its approved charters. Fearing legal challenges, the district sent a letter again demanding that we change our admission policy to comport with the admission policy for all city schools.

They claimed that our review of applicants and lottery process were illegal and violated the principles of neighborhood public schools. We responded in writing to say that Preuss School UCSD was a charter school and was not required to comply with local district policy. Further, our admission policy was elaborately described in the charter school proposal that was approved by their bosses, the San Diego School Board. They did not reply.

Toilet Diplomacy

We were triangulating the merger of three independent and complex bureaucracies during those first years of operation. The San Diego Unified School District followed its own interpretation of the California Education Code; a contradictory document of policies and procedures crafted over a one-hundred year period by politicians, labor unions, and endless lawsuits. Its mass rivals that of the Manhattan White Pages. The University of California, on the other hand, is governed by a device called the University of California Policies and Procedures Manual (PPM). It is, in fact, 18 manuals restricting each campus to uniform practices covering everything from campus real estate transactions to the proper method of ordering water cooler service. The PPM is not so much contradictory as it is oppressive in excruciating detail.

Thirdly, the 1992 California Charter School Act, in contrast to the other two documents, is miniscule in that it spans fewer than a dozen pages. In scope, it is little more than a desire, a sketch, for school reform. The legislation was intentionally brief to allow for maximum freedom, which philosophically ran counter to the school district and university regulations with their penchant for bureaucratic precision and risk avoidance.

From these three administrative control systems, we were fashioning a fourth.

The serious endeavor to design and implement the administrative contours of the Preuss School required great effort tempered with ample amounts of humor. It was a surprise to university academics that all public schools require the construction of two sets of bathrooms, one set for teachers, male and female, and another set for the students. Beyond the humor, the conflict in regulations spoke to the safety issues relating to the difference in size between adults and middle-school children. A former chair of the UCSD chemistry department serving on the Building Advisory Committee argued vociferously for the elimination of 50% of the bathrooms in the new building. It took some time to convince him of the reasons why public school teachers need separate bathrooms. Once he reflected on his own teenage children at home, he was eventually convinced that the authority of teachers in a public school or adults at home could be severely compromised in the eyes of a hormone-ridden adolescent when caught lowering trousers or panty hose in response to the call of nature.

Indeed, bathrooms proved to be a source of much negotiation, compromise, and snickering. The California Education Code directed that the rim of secondary school urinals for students must be no more than 18 inches from the floor, which must be covered with tiles which are no less than one inch and no more than three-and-a-half inches in any direction. But the Preuss School was on university property and was governed by the PPM which required that tile under urinals be eliminated in preference for a painted slab construction. On the UCSD campus all urinals, except for the disabled access units, must be twenty-one inches from the questionable tile. The same conflicts appeared over the height and grip of doorknobs, the placement of windowsills, stairs and railings, as well as the width of walkways. In all cases in construction, we chose to err on the side of safety. Eventually, the new building proved to be a success, and HMC Architects won an AIA award for their design of the building.

Toll and Toil

The sprint to open and run the charter school following the final faculty approval November 1997, however, was taking its toll on me. The dedicated faculty and staff of Thurgood Marshall College were functioning with a half-time provost. By September, the college was welcoming a new crop of entering freshmen, but half of each weekday and all of my weekends were devoted to Preuss School matters. Andrew Sutherland had left and history major, John Lien, had taken his place. For the next two years, John served as Doris' shadow. He developed the student application form and went into the low-income communities with me to describe the school to hopeful parents and recruit students.

Although I had worked with him for the previous two years, it wasn't until one late evening in October at Sherman Elementary School that I learned that he was fluent in Vietnamese. That evening, he had a small cluster of Southeast Asian immigrants in a corner going through the draft application page by page. John seemed to come alive and worked tirelessly preparing presentations and speaking with Latino, African American, and Asian parents in the low-income communities that were the targets of our recruitment efforts. These were tough neighborhoods and he moved easily in and around the countless liquor stores, churches, and schoolyards that frame these communities. The parents trusted him as much as Doris and I trusted him.

Those first two years were a difficult transition for everyone. Doris Alvarez had assumed full control of the operations of the school and her impeccable judgment for teacher quality and training was beginning to pay enormous dividends. Morale was high and the challenge aroused the professional staff. Confirming the mission among some parents and students was proving to be harder, however.

Throughout the application process and orientation both years, families were constantly reminded that the pace and demands of the Preuss School would be unlike those in any public school experience they had encountered. This was particularly true for the eighth grade we admitted in 1999, because they had further to go and less time to prepare to meet the challenge of college admission five years hence. Those students admitted in 1999 scored, on average, at the 55th percentile on standardized tests. Although an imperfect and suspect measurement of academic talent and potential, the tests were an indicator of the distance these motivated young people and their families had to travel. Studies showed that the typical UCSD freshman scored at the 91st percentile on those same national public school tests. There was ample literature and "best guesses" that suggested that we would not, in five years, make up the necessary ground to have these students competitively eligible for selective universities. Although brimming with confidence, we privately wondered if we had not promised too much.

As we began the third year of operation in September 2001, Dick Atkinson had announced his desire to revise UC admission policy with regard to SAT tests. He had often expressed private doubts about the heavy reliance by the University of California upon SAT I tests for admissions. His public doubts threw the historic national debate over standardized aptitude tests into a tailspin. Twenty-two hundred colleges and universities employed SAT I in some form to determine freshman admits; if the University of California were to abandon SAT I, the national repercussions would be enormous. The College Board, which administers millions of these tests each year, was in an uproar and put pressure on Atkinson to recant or moderate his objection.

Preuss School UCSD was built on the premise of helping underrepresented students meet the challenge posed by standardized tests. The uncertain future of the SAT test sent a ripple through our collective thinking. Were the rules changing just as our students were making progress in the standardized testing game? As the date for changes in the SAT evaluation approached, the school persevered with its academic mission as set out in the charter proposal. We had successfully established a high-expectations environment at the Preuss School. Our students were taking trial samples of the SAT I as early as the sixth grade to overcome test anxiety which had been described in the literature as a fundamental barrier to college admissions.

As scholars and politicians debated Atkinson's challenge throughout 2001, Preuss students were settling into the routine, skills, and habits of learning. Families had accepted the "no nonsense" approach that Doris Alvarez insisted upon. The Preuss School was up and running in the hands of a superior academic leader. There were still occasional incidents, but attendance was unusually high, as was teacher morale.

But I was exhausted.

I accepted the invitation to get away for two years to serve as director of the new UC Study Center in London. I left San Diego for London on July 11, 2001 to assume the new assignment. Everyone, including me, thought that this would be an easy post and offer me the opportunity to regularly perform music in Europe. The events of September 11, 2001, however, changed the next two years from a relaxing respite to an international dilemma in study abroad education. Recruiting and orienting students for international education turned what was projected to be a "cushy" job into an international chaotic mess.

Susan Kirkpatrick, professor of Spanish literature, was implored to serve as acting chair of the Preuss School Board of Directors in my two-year absence. She had been associate chancellor and deeply involved since 1997 in the development of the Preuss School, she knew all of the details, and was dedicated to the goals of the new undertaking. Susan was known to be smart, calm, and a progressive in the best sense. She had chaired the UCSD Department of Literature which was famously populated with recalcitrant refugees from the 1960's who were the possessors of aging New Left philosophies. The Preuss School UCSD appealed to her as a common sense approach to the educational aspirations that had brought Third College into existence three decades earlier. She kept in touch with me regularly via e-mail and supported Alvarez effectively. Kirkpatrick experienced the drag of school district staff, but doggedly pushed through the required five-year renewal of the Preuss School charter in early 2002.

Proof in the Pudding

I returned to campus in the summer of 2003 and resumed my duties as provost of Thurgood Marshall College and chair of the Preuss School's board of directors. Much of our time that year was spent preparing for the graduation of the Preuss School's first class of 55 seniors the following June, 2004. Bob Dynes had become the president of the University of California and the UCSD campus was in search of a new chancellor. The campus was now confident of the success of the Preuss School. Anticipating the success of the first graduating class, Bob announced that *he* would be the commencement speaker. Previous enemies and allies of the charter school were now boasting about the wisdom of the project. Bud reminded everyone of the opportunistic social axiom that "success has many parents and failure is an orphan." Preuss School UCSD was no longer an orphan.

We had the right principal, teachers, and support from the parents, and the hard work on the part of everyone was showing results. Bud's research outfit, CREATE, worked diligently to collect and review data. Part One of their 2004 report presented information about Preuss School enrollment trends and student demographics, test scores, course-taking patterns from 1999-2004, and college acceptances for the graduating class of 2004. Part Two presented information about Preuss School students compared to the students who applied for enrollment but were not randomly selected by the lottery to attend.

By academic year 2002-2003, the admissions requirement for low-income students had the effect of selecting a large portion of students from the educationally underserved populations in San Diego County. Indeed, our studies showed that selecting for income allowed the Preuss School UCSD to meet its mission to serve the historically underrepresented students not typically found in the UCSD freshman class. If successful, these students would eventually find their way into the future classes of first-year students attending UCSD and other selective campuses in the system.

The 2004 CREATE Report also observed that, over the years, the African American enrollments at Preuss School UCSD declined from a 1999-2000 high of 24% while Asian enrollments doubled from an original 11% of the total student population.

Given that over 70% of our students were coming from English-learner communities (Spanish, Vietnamese, Cantonese, Hmong, and Khmer), we were pleasantly surprised to note that Preuss students had a high "redesignation" rate; that is, the rate that students are confirmed as English proficient by passing the California English Language Development Test (CELDT). It was clear that the personalized instruction, aided by university tutors, was making a significant difference as compared to the county's "redesignation" rate.

The principal always wanted to hire the very best credentialed teachers. Budget constraints forbade that option, however. Instead, Doris Alvarez devoted a great deal of time and attention to developing younger teachers by assigning a relief period to senior instructors to allow them time to mentor less experienced teachers. It was determined that there would be a truncated schedule on Fridays to permit three hours of professional development activities. By comparison, the average years of experience of teachers at Preuss School were significantly less than for other schools in San Diego County.

Our first commencement day, June 30, 2004, was joyous and weird. Dignitaries gathered in a classroom near the field to don their academic garb. Both Peter and Peggy Preuss made no attempt to contain their ebullient mood. Peter generously hugged everyone who entered the room; he didn't speak, he gushed with the pride of a newly minted grandfather. His thick German accent was even more unintelligible than usual, but no one cared; we just enjoyed him enjoying the success of the kids.

Doris and her staff organized the day brilliantly. Beaming eleventh-graders welcomed celebrants in the parking lot, colorful balloons marked the path to the outdoor site and served as metaphor for the longer journey parents and family members had completed to arrive at this moment and place. Doris scampered in and out of the room checking on every detail of the ceremony. She greeted dignitaries in between clipped sentences hurled into either her cell phone in one hand or her walkie-talkie in the other.

Dr. Doris Alvarez
Photo / Melissa Jacobs

I watched her in deep admiration and was reminded of her response on the bright sunny Tuesday a year earlier when one of our yellow buses loaded with 30-plus students overturned on the freeway. That day, she stood in the middle of Interstate-5 with the California Highway Patrol and ambulance services tending to the children, coordinating the staff back at the school, contacting parents, and informing the press. The scene reminded me of the famous statement by Dr. Martin Luther King, Jr. in *Strength to Love*, when he said that: "The ultimate measure of a man [or woman] is not where he [or she] stands in moments of comfort and convenience, but where he [or she] stands at times of challenge and controversy." The sight of this two-fisted communicator standing in the middle of a California freeway tending to her kids convinced me that we had chosen the right person to lead this unique demonstration project.

Alan Bersin, superintendent of the San Diego Unified School District, entered the room with little fanfare. He had been a reluctant supporter of the Preuss School six years earlier. But, as with all good politicians, he was not going to miss an opportunity to share credit for the success of the school. He and a nemesis of his serving on the San Diego Board of Education rotated in opposite directions around the punch bowl and cookies.

Dynes arrived late with his entourage from the UC Office of the President. He stood for pictures with everyone in the room and greeted parents as they walked past. He was as proud as he was relieved.

Parents and family members stopped at various points between the parking lot and the field to celebrate, hug their kids, relentlessly giggle, and share their smiles. Scores of small children chased the colorful balloons that caromed off shoulders and feet as the swelling crowd rushed to take their seats. The noisy open-air amphitheater in the courtyard was filled with hundreds of visitors in anticipation of the graduation. The air was filled with Spanish, Vietnamese, Somali, Khmer, and a plethora of other happy voices under a sunny late afternoon sky, typical of San Diego in the summer. Pairs of F-14 Tomcat fighters from nearby Miramar Air Station, almost on cue, roared overhead to open the ceremony. They, too, added to the festive atmosphere.

Doris selected seven graduating seniors to open the ceremony with a brief welcome in seven different languages: English, Spanish, German, Vietnamese, Cambodian, Swahili, and Hawaiian. Bob Dynes was impressed by the academic performance of the graduating students and the array of top-notch colleges and universities that accepted Preuss School graduates for entrance the following fall. He was also deeply moved by the spectacle of the event. Bob was center stage in the shadow of the gleaming Preuss School UCSD, surrounded by hundreds of proud parents and family members, network television cameras, and a multitude of curious onlookers. In his remarks, he spoke of the campus debate and the roles he and I both played in creating the institution. Preuss School UCSD opened on his watch; it was the singular achievement of his seven years as chancellor of the UC San Diego campus.

Each member on the dais approached the podium to deliver prepared remarks. Peter Preuss gushed with a "papa's" pride. He had made a difference and he had given back in a unique, precedent-setting way. Fran Zimmerman spoke on behalf of the San Diego School Board and took a one-line swipe at Alan Bersin. For his part, Alan remarked on the value of public education and how Preuss School UCSD was pointing the way towards the reforms necessary for public schools. Doris wisely recognized the sacrifices of the parents and teachers supporting these young people, who began each morning as early as 5:30 A.M. preparing to catch yellow school buses for the trip north up Interstate-5 to the UCSD campus in La Jolla.

When my five minutes came, I reminded the graduating seniors of their first year at Preuss School in those temporary bungalows and muddy walkways on the Thurgood Marshall College campus. I asked their parents to reflect on their feelings that first year. They trusted us to protect and teach their children, even though it was my belief that UCSD had not earned their trust at that point.

As each one of the seniors crossed the stage, the outdoor audience roared their approval. Parents cheered for their children and themselves. They had good reason to believe that their child's short walk across the stage was symbolic of their intergenerational journey out of poverty, disenfranchisement, and marginalization. The students' success was proof of their success, their well-earned victory. Both the students and their families had taken a chance on UCSD and themselves to confirm Bill McGill's tenacious belief in what was, or could be, good in America.

This day was a commencement and a culmination. Like thousands of other high school seniors in San Diego that month, these 55 youngsters were receiving diplomas marking the end of their secondary education. They had outperformed the comparison cohort, their siblings and friends attending other public schools. They were academically better prepared than most graduates in the state, regardless of socio-economic status. They were fully prepared to begin the next stage in their personal development.

Preuss School UCSD had intervened in the trajectory of their lives and invited them to join and gradually reconfigure a new kind of aristocracy. Not the aristocracy of mandarin upstarts. These Preuss graduates were not born into and cultivated by middle and upper-middle class families who exploited every possible opportunity to expand their franchise and fortune. They were not "born on third base" and declared to have hit a triple. These courageous young people had clawed their way uphill onto the field of play and brought with them the knowledge, customs, beliefs, and values of people born at the margins of an American mainstream that had no place for them to stand, let alone score homeruns.

Although remarkable, they were not unusual. Preuss School UCSD set out to demonstrate that children typically found in the urban public schools of America can achieve at a very high level if the adults in their schools and in their lives set high standards and provide the intellectual and social "scaffolds" that Bud wrote about.

Some of the UCSD faculty in attendance saw the day as the culmination of a gamble. They recognized that every participant at the Preuss School had worked extremely hard to produce astounding educational results with kids who were not expected to do astounding things. Some felt that we "got lucky" or "dodged a bullet" and could not repeat the achievement here or replicate the model elsewhere. But, indeed, the seventy-five graduates the following year exceeded the achievements of the 2004 class with acceptances to Harvard, Stanford, Penn, Berkeley, UCLA, and, yes, UCSD, earning a total of more than $800,000 in merit scholarship awards.

The Preuss School model was secure in its approach and fully capable of graduating competitively eligible students each year. Bud and I were convinced, further, that the model could be translated to almost any school, in any neighborhood. It would take a dedicated and inspired teaching staff, supportive families, and major transformations in how a particular public school functions. The innovations of a longer school day and year, individualized instruction, university tutors, and a single-track college preparatory curriculum all contributed to the success of the model. The thing that could not be measured or easily reproduced was the salutary benefit of attending secondary school on a university campus. Could this model be transplanted to a neighborhood public school in the communities from which these students came?

It was clear to us that the real test of the Preuss School UCSD would involve developing the model in "real-time" at a local inner-city school with all of the vagaries of the neighborhood and absent the "halo" effect of being on the university campus.

Despite the anguished birth pangs, Preuss School UCSD was receiving national recognition for establishing a daring approach to changing the educational outcome of students historically underrepresented at the University of California. We had taken the first tremulous steps toward effectively meeting the burden of our excellence. Although more than a symbolic gesture, the Preuss School UCSD alone could not meet the challenge of creating a sufficient critical mass of local ethnic minority students, fully eligible to be accepted at UCSD.

Eternally restless, we were already looking at Gompers Middle School and Lincoln High School in southeast San Diego as possible sites to transplant the best practices that made the Preuss School UCSD successful.

But that effort would encounter a very different set of proponents, opponents, stressors, and opportunities. This time, however, we would take with us into the community a well-earned trust and demonstrated capability to meet our burden and obligations.

Acknowledgements

The Burden of Excellence emerges from many different inspirations. Lacey P. Lytle, my father, was the best janitor in Harlem and instilled in me a passion for passion. The pride he took in his work was evident and meaningful. Carrying his tool box up and down the stairs of the tenements he oversaw at 468 West 148th Street, he taught his aspiring young son to take pride in menial as well as grand work.

Some evenings, he would sit up late at night copying out the *Chorale Preludes* of Johannes Sebastian Bach, to place his rough hewn hand along side that of true genius, to experience what it felt like to travel along the path of creativity.

Mom was a genius of the other sort. She was capable of organizing the creative energies of a rookery of ten children, plus neighbor friends, on behalf of their collective salvation. A very holy woman, Margaret Ethel Lytle with her fifth-grade education successfully met the daily challenges, despite the dire poverty that gripped our family before, during, and following World War II. It was Mama Harris, her mother, who taught us to sing and recite the hymn, *Brighten the Corner Where You're At*.

Taken together Lacey and Margaret Lytle are the recipients envisioned in the creation of Preuss School UCSD. They were the industrious, kind, and hard-working people who would have run through any door opened on their behalf. They provided an "education home" where each child was encouraged to pursue high school graduation and college. All did, including four with doctoral degrees, a math professor, a judge, engineers—good people all.

Rebecca Lytle was there for thirty years to remind me of how blessed we were to have two very bright and healthy children. Our fortune, she believed, was rooted in the legacy of the American work ethic we both inherited, and in the hope that even the meek, with the provision of an "opened door," can compete with the strong. Her life, like her death, provided inspiration for the establishment of Preuss School UCSD.

Most of all and most recently, the courage, optimism, and hard work of the families of Preuss School UCSD remind me that the opening of doors is the responsibility and burden of public institutions—a burden that must be taken up by all of us.

For more information about ongoing efforts to establish urban Educational Field Stations throughout California and the nation, please visit the Center for Research on Educational Equity, Assessment, and Teaching Excellence (CREATE) web site:

http://create.ucsd.edu/

www.ingramcontent.com/pod-product-compliance
Lightning Source LLC
LaVergne TN
LVHW051837080426
835512LV00018B/2933